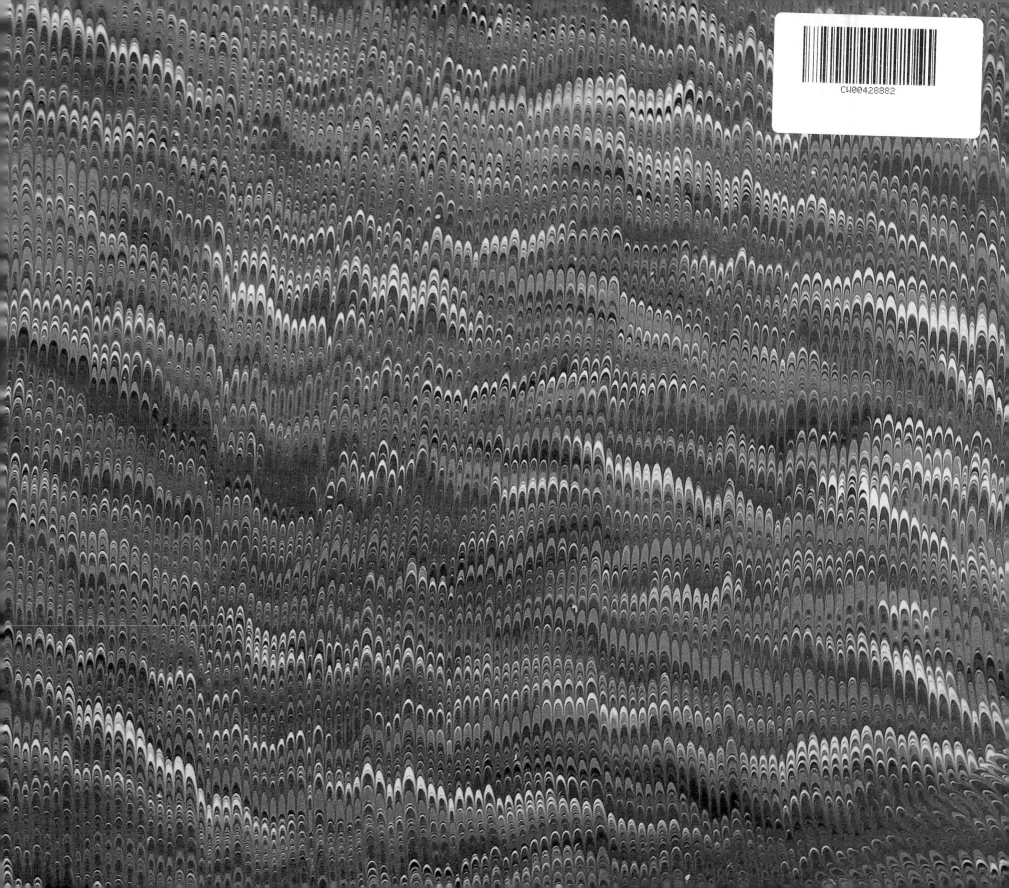

Significant Figures
In Art and Craft Today

Portraits of working artists and craftsmen in Britain

Derek Reay

Foreword by David Linley

Published in 2011 by MoTi Publishing, UK
All photographs copyright Derek Reay

Printed in China on behalf of Latitude Press Limited

ISBN 978-0-9556154-3-6

Profits from this book are being donated to Diabetes UK, Registered Charity No 215199

Books by the same author:
Pinhole Photography - The Art and Practice (2008)
Windsor People - 100 People who make Windsor Work (2008)

www.derekreayphotography.co.uk

Acknowledgements

I would like to thank all those artists and craftsmen who have been so generous in their support, given me their time, and welcomed me into their places of work and their homes. Whilst practically all the photographs were taken in workshops and studios, some of the commissioned work was located elsewhere and photographed with the agreement of the owners/ curators. My thanks are therefore extended to the following for granting their permission:

The Victoria & Albert Museum, London, for the fish server which forms part of the Rabinovitch collection of contemporary fish and cake servers (page 26); Professor Liversey for the ladies' brooch (page 26); The Taigh Chearsabhagh Museum & Arts Centre, North Uist, hosts of Chris Drury's exhibition (pages 44-45); Birmingham City Council for the tree carvings at Ley Hill Park, Northfield, Birmingham (pages 54-55); Dudley Metropolitan Borough Council and The Friends of Stevens Park, Wollescote, for the tree carving (page 54); Standard Chartered Bank Plc, London, for 'Girl Walking' (page 98); The Chapter of Salisbury Cathedral for stonemasonry (pages 104-105); Mr and Mrs Walley of Coton House Farm, Coton, Shropshire, for hedge laying work (pages 130-1); Buckingham Palace for access to the Royal Mews (pages 152-3) and Katherine Brett for the use of her marbled paper design as the end papers of this book.

Most of all I would like to thank my wife Eileen who spent many late nights editing the texts and gave constant support.

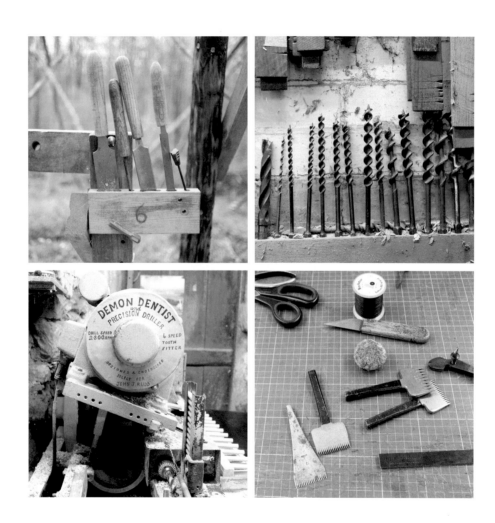

Contents

Foreword

The words 'craftsmanship' and 'British' evoke the strongest of sentiments within me. I was therefore delighted and honoured to be asked to introduce Derek Reay's book. I should add that Derek himself is an accomplished craftsman in his own right, which I think is self evident from the style and execution of what you see to follow.

Through my own training as a cabinet maker I have been privileged to meet many skilled people within this particular sphere. My own experience has left me acutely aware of the great wealth of talent we have in this country, and even more so of the challenges we face as a nation in preserving these skills and carrying them into the next generation. However even I was delighted and surprised by the sheer variety and breadth of crafts and disciplines that this book entails, all of which - for the time being anyway - are still prevalent within the UK today. From the last remaining practitioners of their craft, such as the wood block maker (Chris Daunt) and the bow hair dresser (Michael Sowden) through to the only living blacksmith to hold a gold medal (Bob Hobbs), there is a plethora of talent and artistic endeavour.

Derek's work covers the widest range possible, from rural crafts that are little known outside their region to the more established and well-known art and crafts. He has travelled the length and the breadth of the British Isles and captured people in their varied and interesting work environments.

This book is more than a tribute to people who have achieved significance in the pursuit of their art or craft. It is a genuine celebration. Derek has meticulously and sympathetically captured not only the achievements and skills of those included, but conveys through his work the strength of personality and passion of the individuals he has chosen to feature. It is not merely a visual journey but a tour de force, showing the determination and love of their craft that all these practitioners share. It is this that has made them the craftsmen of today.

'Significant Figures' rejoices in the skills of craftsmanship. It also serves as a prescient reminder of the need to encourage the British government and Education Authorities to nurture the skills of such trades in the younger generation and thus preserve them for our children and children's children.

All profits from Derek's book are being donated to the charity Diabetes UK.

David Linley 2010

Introduction

Over the last few years I have photographed many people in their working or social environments. This is an aspect of photography that particularly interests me. For as long as I can remember I have had a love of art and crafts, so it seemed appropriate to produce a photographic record of the lives and work of those who make these wonderful pieces. The result is this book.

This collection of photographs and accompanying texts attempts to show not only the individual artists and craftsmen in their workshops or studios, but also seeks to explain the main features of their art or craft. My quest has taken me to the far reaches of England, Scotland and Wales. Without exception everyone wholeheartedly embraced the idea of this project and was very welcoming. I have travelled across the sea, made long motorway journeys and driven down countless by-roads and farm tracks. I have met some amazing people and been privileged to learn about their world. I do not claim to have included all disciplines, but have tried to incorporate as wide a range of art and craft as possible; something which, as far as I am aware, has not been attempted before within a single book. In some cases I have included more than one example within a craft, in order to show different end products; some intended for practical use, others as decorative art. For example, one of the willow weavers builds sculptures, the other makes coffins. In the book, I have grouped people into broad categories and, within these, arranged the participants alphabetically.

Traditional crafts are often specific to a geographical area. Many of these have a strong following and have seen something of a revival. For example, demand for willow coffins has increased in recent years as people become more aware of their environment. Many craftsmen, particularly those involved with rural crafts, run courses to teach others and pass on their skills.

In their different ways, each person featured has made an impact within their sphere of art or craft. Many have achieved high honour within their Guild, Association or Worshipful Company, and have gained peer recognition. Most pursue their craft professionally, some having reached the highest level of commercial success. In a few cases they represent the last remaining people practising their craft in this country; they are the last of their line.

The main photographs show the craftsman or woman at work, although in a few cases, more formal portraiture seemed appropriate. Supplementary photographs show other aspects of their work, and in many cases, the finished products.

Perhaps we should stop to think about who will follow in their footsteps. Almost everyone photographed could trace their interest back to childhood - the comment was often made that the person "liked making things", they had a practical bent. Several joined the family firm, others went to art school and recall specific events or people who inspired them and effectively directed their future careers. Yet others became apprenticed and formally learnt the craft from Masters. A few literally stumbled upon their craft by accident, taking a job that happened to come along, and finding it to their liking. We must hope that future governments will seek to achieve a good balance between academic and practical training, and thereby influence the public perception of the value of craftsmanship to society.

In 2008 I photographed *100 People Who Make Windsor Work* documenting many of the trades and professions within the community. Originally intended as an exhibition for the Windsor Fringe Festival, I was persuaded to publish it. A comment made at the time was that it served as an interesting social documentary. It is my hope that this book will do the same.

Sadly, just before this book went to press, I learned that John Randall, Master Bowyer, had died after a long illness. However, it was agreed with his family and his colleague Alan Rogers that the text, to which he contributed, should remain unchanged.

Bruce Aitken - Clockmaker

Bruce is a self-taught clockmaker. He has a background in engineering, electronics and more recently, design and technology teaching. His love of construction stems from early childhood, as does a fascination with the inner workings of machinery. Making interesting clocks with exposed mechanisms has occupied him intermittently since the early 1980s. In 1990, the chance discovery of an old photograph of a strange and beautiful clock made entirely from wood captured his imagination and led indirectly to his change of career.

Wood has been used as a material for clock making since medieval times. The development of wooden geared clocks broadly paralleled that of metal ones until comparatively recent times; both types were high status items, embodying the finest technology available. During the first quarter of the eighteenth century, the illustrious clockmakers John and James Harrison created precision clocks made largely from wood - at that time they were amongst the most accurate clocks in the world. A few examples are still functioning today. In 19th century Connecticut, Eli Terry was making reliable wooden clocks on an industrial scale, having pioneered the development of modern production methods.

Wood is a challenging material for clock making - it is not uniformly strong and it changes shape with both temperature and humidity. Bruce has worked hard to be certain that the design of each element allows the wood to move as it needs to without affecting the overall running of the clock. He also uses a variety of techniques to ensure that wear is kept to an absolute minimum: microscopic inspection shows no wear in clocks that have run for several years. Modern materials are incorporated, replacing the now endangered tropical hardwood used by the Harrisons and others for making pivots.

The heart of a mechanical clock is the escapement - Bruce employs the Graham Deadbeat, a particularly elegant system invented around 1715. The escapement transfers energy from a slowly descending weight via a train of gear wheels to the pendulum, maintaining its oscillations. The pendulum in turn regulates the speed of rotation of the wheels, enabling the clock to display the correct time. The deadbeat escapement is well suited to wooden clocks, being much more efficient than previous types.

Bruce's workshop is part of the old tram depot in Matlock, a well-lit space with large windows. He has a wide variety of tools, many of which have been significantly modified for clockmaking. In addition to designing the clocks, he has also devised the processes used to make them and is constantly adapting these methods to further improve their operation and appearance.

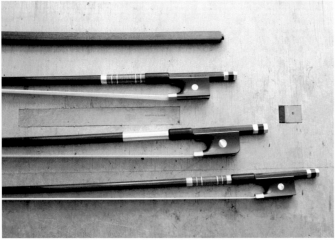

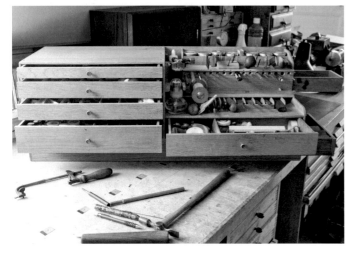

Tim Baker - Violin Bow Maker

Tim Baker graduated with distinction from the Newark School of Violin Making in 1981, and joined W.E. Hill & Sons where he trained as a bowmaker and repairer. In 1984 he joined J&A Beare Ltd, where his time was divided between bow making, restoration and the study of old bows. With the encouragement of Charles Beare, he has developed a special interest in English bows dating from 1750 and has given a number of lectures on the subject both in the USA and Europe. He was a major contributor to *The British Violin*, published by the British Violin Making Association.

In 1992 he was invited to join the jury of the bowmaking competition at the Manchester International Cello Festival, and has returned several times. He has also judged competitions in Paris and the USA. More recently, he has been involved with the Oberlin Summer School in Ohio, and in 2006 worked with colleagues to establish a similar professional development course at West Dean College here in the UK. Since the end of 2000, he has worked independently, concentrating on bowmaking whilst retaining a close association with J&A Beare. His bows are strongly influenced by the mid 19th century French makers, in particular the Peccatte School.

Tim makes violin, viola and cello bows. Violin and viola bows are the same length and weigh 60 and 70 grammes respectively. The length of hair needed to hair the bow is 29 inches (horse hair is sold in bundles of different lengths) although, in order to be able to adequately secure the hair to the bow, a length of 30 or 32 inches, is used, the longer length making the job easier. The cello bow is usually some 30 mm (approx. 1 inch) shorter and weighs approximately 80 grammes. When making a bow, Tim believes the selection of wood is the single most important consideration. Like all quality bow makers he uses pernambuco, a Brazilian wood having dense orange heartwood which is both reflective and resilient. This makes bows with good playing qualities, allowing the musician to draw the optimum sound from their instrument.

Users of Tim's bows include soloists, orchestral and chamber musicians, as well as a number of teachers in leading Conservatoires and their students.

An in-depth article on Tim Baker was published in 'The Strad' magazine in May 2004.

Chris Daunt - Wood Block Maker

Chris studied Fine Art at Newcastle Polytechnic, was a Cistercian monk in the Scottish Borders for four years, obtained an English degree from Newcastle University, and taught English in Poland for a year. However, Chris was, and is, primarily a freelance wood engraver. When he began wood engraving it seemed natural for him to make his own engraving blocks since his brother was a woodworker and allowed him to use his workshop.

In 1993 the family firm of T N Lawrence, who had been making blocks for the engraving trade since the 1860s, announced its intention to stop the manufacture of end-grain engraving blocks. This situation threatened the continuation of wood engraving as an art form and the Society of Wood Engravers became very concerned. The then President of the Society, Hilary Paynter, was aware that Chris made his own blocks and asked if he would take over wood block making as a business. He agreed; the Society bought him the required machinery and hand tools, and he is now the only supplier in the UK, with many customers world-wide. It is particularly interesting to note that Chris lives and works on Tyneside, just across the river from where Thomas Bewick started the modern practice of wood engraving over 200 years ago.

Blocks are traditionally made from boxwood (buxus sempervirens), a slow growing indigenous hardwood. Box is the hardest and heaviest of the native hardwoods and is evergreen, a great advantage as the growth rings are constant throughout the year and do not have the seasonal variations of deciduous woods, which produce rings of varying hardness. As all engraving is made on the end-grain this is extremely important. Lemonwood is also used, a wood whose citrus-smelling sap gives it its name. In the USA maple is used as box does not grow in that country.

Chris buys his logs from woodsmen at various estates around the country. Box grows to a diameter of 4-6 inches, seldom more, although he has some very old logs whose diameter is about 15 inches. The logs are cut into slices about 1 inch thick and seasoned for at least two years. Due to their small diameter, and because the wood needs be free from any imperfections, only about 50% is usable. Blocks are therefore made from a number of small pieces, up to 2 inches square, to achieve the required size. All blocks are made to order, their size ranging from about 2 inches square (a single piece) to a composite up to 8 x 10 inches. Pieces are cut out, their sides carefully planed and glued together. The surfaces are milled to a thickness of 0.918 inches, the exact size for letterpress printing, before being scraped and polished to give a perfect surface. For a composite block Chris always ensures that the individual pieces come from the same log to maximise their thermal stability and ensure a consistent density across the block. The joints and surface finish must be absolutely perfect and scratch free since any imperfections in the block will appear on the print.

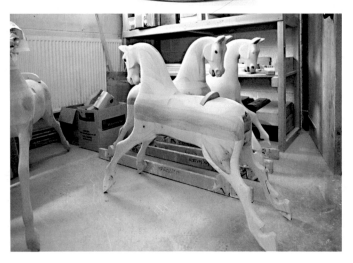

Anthony Dew - Rocking Horse Maker

Anthony's early years were spent at sea as a navigator, after which he attended college, intending to study mathematics. In fact, he studied art and soon turned to wood carving, which, in his final year, required him to work on a specific project. Although he knew nothing about horses, he decided to carve a rocking horse and the result attracted a great deal of nostalgic interest - and he satisfied his examiners. The thought then occurred to him that this might be an enjoyable way of making a living - and his business was formed. However, in those early years he also taught woodworking whilst the business became fully established. He is now President of the Guild of Rocking Horse Makers, which has 1350 members worldwide. Qualification for membership is that the person must have made their own rocking horse.

The heyday for rocking horses was between 1880 and 1930, after which it tended to lose popularity. However, Anthony has successfully revived the craft and his horses are now sold throughout the world. All the components are made in his workshop. He makes a wide range of horses although most customers prefer the older styles. Every one is hand carved, every horse is different. If a customer has any special requirement, this can be accommodated; for example, a particular colour to match an owner's live horse. All the horses have real horsehair manes and tails. One customer even asked for a replica of his deceased horse, and wanted to use the actual mane and tail hair! Yet another requested a horse made to a size that would "just fit the alcove". In the main picture, Anthony is working on his largest horse to date - which will measure 20 ft long and 16ft high. Occasionally a horse returns for renovation, often 20 or 30 years after it was first bought. He has in the past made fairground horses, but these tend to have their saddles as an integral part of the carving and are not traditional rocking horses. Anthony sells directly from his workshop in Yorkshire, never through other retail outlets. He also supplies DIY kits.

He also uses a number of different types of wood, the most common being tulip wood which, in addition to carving well and having a good appearance, is a plantation grown hardwood and therefore from renewable sources. The stands and rockers are made from ash, or sometimes chestnut. Early horses had bow shaped rockers made from solid timber, but in 1880 a swinging iron stand was patented which had the decided advantage of being able to rock the horse without it moving along the floor and possibly trampling on toes. Most horses now use the iron stand.

The oldest known rocking horse was made for Prince Charles in 1605 in order to teach him to ride. A few years ago Anthony made the Victoria and Albert Museum of Childhood aware of the whereabouts of that actual horse and they were able to purchase it. Not surprisingly it was fragile and, in 2000, he made a replica which was displayed in the museum alongside the original (see centre picture).

Christoph Götting - Violin Maker

Christoph was born in Wiesbaden, Germany, in 1948 to a musical family. Between 1964 and 1967 he served his apprenticeship at the long established School of Violin Making in Mittenwald, Germany. In 1969 he joined the prestigious workshops of J. & A. Beare in London, where he stayed until 1990. During a break in 1974 he obtained his Master Diploma in Mittenwald for which he received a Gold Medal. He rejoined the Beare workshop and became one of their principal craftsmen. During his time at Beares' he was privileged to restore and study numerous Stradivari violins and many other priceless antique instruments.

Christoph's workshop is a converted granary in Michelmersh, Hampshire, and looks out over gentle farmland. I visited him on a cold sunny winter's day and spent a most interesting time discussing his working methods. Christoph makes violins and violas in a very traditional handcrafted way. He is very much aware that the violin is a rare object that can be improved only by looking back in time and by studying the best old examples of the craft. That is why he has spent countless hours on varnish research and experiments. He is convinced that his varnish closely resembles the classical varnishes of the 18th Century and considers this to be the key to achieving the ultimate quality of sound and appearance of his instruments.

He has so far avoided making antique looking reproductions; in his opinion the appearance of his work resembles the look of classical instruments at a stage when they were nearly new. Christoph's violins bear the label: Christoph Götting Mattiacensis, fecit Michelmershii anno 20... 'Mattiacensis' is Latin for 'from Wiesbaden', 'fecit Michelmershii' means: 'made in Michelmersh'.

He uses various woods for his instruments; in particular, mountain-grown maple for most of the sound box, except for the 'table' (the front), which is made from fine grained mountain spruce, chosen for its superb resonance. Apart from the highest violin string, E, which is nearly always made from pure steel, Christoph uses both gut core and plastic core strings, although his preference is for gut core. All modern gut core strings (apart from plain strings used for true baroque instruments) are wound with aluminium or silver in order to achieve a brighter, louder sound. Christoph does not make bows as this is a specialist craft in its own right.

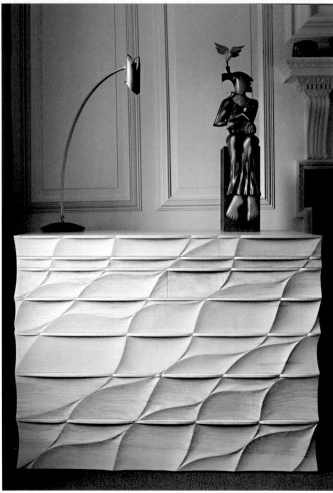

Top: Cabinet veneered in holly and black oak. Bottom: Chest in ripple ash.
Right: Table also in ripple ash, both using wood from the same tree.

John Makepeace - Furniture Designer and Maker

John's childhood home contained furniture made by his paternal grandfather and certain pieces made a very strong impression. At the age of eleven he visited the workshop of Hugh Birkett whose style he remembers as being dated but whose workmanship he greatly admired. In the 1960's a family friend suggested he should go to Scandinavia to visit the furniture makers of Copenhagen; he was immediately struck by the excitement of furniture design, quality, and how each maker would carefully guard his piece until unveiled at the annual exhibition. John set up his own design and furniture making business; his natural ability earning him widespread professional recognition. This led to his appointment as a design consultant to the All India Handicraft Board, to being a founder member of the Crafts Council in the UK and a Trustee of the V&A. Many commissions followed including several Oxford Colleges and Liberty of London. Major museums as well as private customers saw his potential and acquired his work.

John felt strongly that craftsmen lacked a sense of professionalism and that their ability to run their businesses was not in keeping with their craft skills; he realised there was a balance needed between design, production and business management. In 1976 he bought Parnham House in Dorset and started his school of furniture, alongside but separate from, his own business. The course followed a two year programme, each year's intake being limited to eleven students. National and international visiting lecturers added a unique dimension and Parnham rapidly gained an enviable reputation. Following the sale of Parnham in 2001 John moved into Beaminster where he has his design studio, gallery and timber seasoning sheds. In 1982, as Director of the Parnham Trust which ran the school at Parnham, he purchased a 350 acre woodland and raised the funds to develop and demonstrate the new timber technologies. These were developed through the European programme of collaborative research he initiated to explore the better utilisation of timber. In 2000 John handed over to a new director who oversaw the amalgamation of the enterprise with the Architectural Association.

His inspiration comes from a keen observation of the world around him, from ancient buildings to living plants. He is strongly influenced by form and shape, exemplified by his table in the main photograph whose design is called 'Vault'. John thinks deeply about how a piece of furniture will be used; it must be beautiful yet fulfil its purpose without compromise. He uses only English woods. He utilises the colour and grain of the wood to great artistic effect and his design is not determined by machine processes but by the forms best suited to their purpose. He uses woods with exceptional character, some recent pieces made from holly, ripple ash, black oak, yew and mulberry. He now concentrates on the design of furniture and works with independent craftsmen, all of whom have been members of his studio and who now have their own workshops.

John was awarded an OBE in 1988 for services to furniture design and in 2002 he received the American Furniture Society's Award of Distinction. In May 2010 he received a Lifetime Achievement Award from The Worshipful Company of Furniture Makers and in October of the same year was nominated for the Prince Philip Designers Prize.

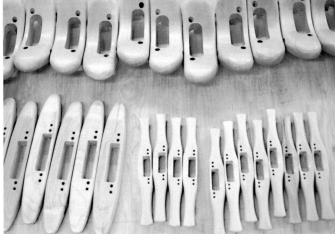

James Mursell
Windsor Chair Maker

As a hobby, James made several rocking chairs and soon realised that his preference was for the more fluid forms of woodwork rather than the right angles and flat surfaces required of cabinet-making. He was introduced to Windsor chairs by Jack Hill at West Dean and regards this as a life-changing experience; within an hour he realised this suited him absolutely. Machine made chairs with their inherent uniformity had no character, they were lifeless. Hand-made chairs were individuals, each spindle slightly different, each curve unique.

In the 1990's his fruit growing business underwent a change when, almost overnight, the change in Sunday trading laws resulted in weekend fruit-pickers finding it easier to go to the supermarket. James now devotes all his time to Windsor chair making as a business. He has no regrets. Having learnt all he could in this country, he turned to America and studied under Mike Dunbar, a leading exponent of the craft. He toured New England, where he learned about many different forms of the chair.

James now runs courses both at West Dean and at The Windsor Workshop, his own spacious premises where up to six students learn the craft and produce a Windsor chair of their choice. He is the author of *Windsor Chairmaking* published in 2009.

The golden age of Windsor chairs was between 1720 and 1800. From a low point at the beginning of the 20th century, interest in these chairs has increased significantly. A Windsor chair has a solid seat into which pieces of wood are inserted to form the legs and the back - these are not connected other than through the seat. The seat is traditionally made from elm, a wood not normally used by cabinet makers on account of its instability but which is ideal for the Windsor chair. The seat is generally constructed from a single plank of wood before cutting, drilling and shaping. The legs and spindles are typically made from ash which splits well and is easily available. The legs are turned on the lathe. The back, or bow, is steam-bent into shape. James makes his spindles from green wood - wood which has not been seasoned - these being individually shaped using hand-tools, many of which he makes himself using a design which gives him maximum control of the shape of the chair.

Lawrence Neal
Rush Seated Chair Maker

Lawrence is the latest in a long line of traditional rush seated chair makers operating since the middle of the 19th century, when Philip Clissett started making chairs in Herefordshire in 1838. Philip taught Ernest Gimson who revived the ancient craft of making ash chairs with rush seats as part of the Arts and Crafts movement in 1890. He established his workshop in Daneway, Gloucestershire, where he encouraged a local young man, Edward Gardiner, to take up chair making. In 1939 Neville Neal joined Edward as a pupil and, when Edward died in 1958, Neville moved the workshop to its present location in the village of Stockton in Warwickshire. In 1966, his son Lawrence joined his father as an apprentice and, following his father's death in 2000, continued to make these traditional chairs in the same workshop. Most of the chairs were designed by Gimson whose aim was to show that well-designed and skilfully made chairs by village craftsmen were comparable with the best of the products of the old chair makers.

There are more people making rush seated chairs now than was the case a few years ago but, according to Lawrence, few do it well. His father always maintained that you had to produce a hundred chairs before you could begin to make a good one - the skill is in the neatness and symmetry of both the frame and the seat. Only local materials are used: English oak and ash, plus locally sourced rushes. The oak is obtained from a timber yard where logs are specifically chosen by Lawrence. Ash is sourced from around Worcester and Malvern; 20 to 30 year old trees of approximately 9 inch diameter being chosen; such trees are too small to be stocked by timber yards. All the wood is cut and split in the workshop and turned on the lathe as required.

Wooden patterns, many over a hundred years old, are used to indicate where the joints are to be cut, different patterns being used for each chair design. Although the spars and slats are made from dry timber, the legs are used green so that after the chair is assembled the shrinkage in the legs helps to tighten the joints. It is said that chair makers in the past did not use glue and relied solely on this shrinkage but nowadays modern glues are used.

Lawrence collects enough common bulrushes from the banks of the rivers Avon or Leam during a two week period in June or July. This is a years' supply, although they can be stored indefinitely. Before use, the rushes are soaked overnight and covered to prevent them from drying out while working. When weaving the seat, a number of rush strands are twisted together to give strength.

Top: Fish server from the Rabinovitch collection.
Bottom: Armorial bearings of a Master Apothecary as depicted on his Lady's brooch.
Both items made for private clients.

Alan Mudd - Enameller

Following his studies in Fine Art, Alan took the only job available at the time and served an apprenticeship as an engraver in the textile industry where he engraved rollers used for printing textiles. After completing his National Service he returned to find the factory had closed as new methods of printing on fabrics, such as photogravure, were being introduced. He moved to London and joined the specialist enamelling workshop of C F Barnes who supplied the jewellery trade. Starting as an engraver, Alan trained as an enameller using traditional techniques. He stayed with the company for over twenty years during which time he became a partner in the business. He now works independently from his studio in Norfolk. He is a founder member and a Fellow of the Institute of Professional Goldsmiths, a Freeman of the Worshipful Company of Goldsmiths and has worked as a part-time lecturer at Middlesex University.

Enamel is a combination of quartz and soda ash with additional metallic oxides which give the glass its colour. The basic principle of the craft involves creating cells on a surface and filling them with enamel. There are several types of enamelling, distinguished by the differences in the way the cells are created.

Champlevé is the technique of hand carving with scorpers to create the cells of the metal object - usually silver or gold; Guilloché is a technique using an engine turning machine. Cloisonné refers to the technique of creating the cells by first gluing silver or gold wires onto a metal substrate and then soldering them together. A further technique is called Plique á Jour (French for 'braid letting in daylight') where the design may also be formed from wires, or pierced out of a sheet of metal; in this case it is placed onto a temporary sheet of platinum foil which is ultimately peeled off to reveal a stained glass window effect.

Alan concentrates on the Champlevé and Plique á Jour methods, the former being practised by Genevan enamellers to make luxury objects. In all cases the cells are individually filled with powdered enamel of the required colour and the whole piece fired in a kiln for a few minutes to allow the glass to melt and fuse to the metal. It is then removed from the furnace and allowed to cool to room temperature. This process may be repeated up to 5 or 6 times adding more coats of glass in order to produce the required quality. In the case of Plique á Jour the next step is the removal of the temporary platinum base resulting in a beautiful translucent object. There is then a final process of lapping and polishing in order to complete the article.

Although utilitarian enamelled articles are manufactured in large factories, artistic objects are invariably produced by individuals or very small groups of artists.

Carl Nordbruch - Glass Artist

Centre and Right: Peter Riley with Carl Nordbruch.

After leaving school Carl was offered two jobs – one involving pest control; the other glass blowing. Having little idea of what was involved with either he chose glass blowing as it was better paid. Events were to prove his choice correct; his innate ability allowing his skills to flourish. He served an apprenticeship at the Isle of Wight Glass Company where he learnt from Peter Riley. He was then invited to reinvigorate the glass department of the University of Wolverhampton which he did with such enthusiasm that every student became involved with glass blowing. On leaving Wolverhampton, he obtained a Masters degree at the Royal College of Art after which he set up his present company with his former mentor Peter Riley. They specialise in commissions for a wide range of architects and designers serving a world-wide market. Carl loves the art of glass blowing because it is instant - the results can be seen within hours, which suits his personality. He is regularly invited to exhibit, his reputation being spread entirely by word of mouth.

The raw material is 24% lead crystal from Dartington in Devon. His furnace holds a reservoir of 63 litres of molten glass which lasts about two days before replenishment. To create an object the blow-pole is inserted into the furnace and a fixed pear-shaped quantity of glass adheres to its end; this is withdrawn whilst constantly being rotated to ensure the molten glass remains on the end of the pole. Depending on the size of the finished artefact - and Carl specialises in some large pieces - more glass may be needed, in which case the blow-pole and glass is reinserted into the furnace. This process may be repeated several times until the desired mass of glass is obtained, a situation determined by the final size and thickness of the finished product. The glass is then inserted into a second furnace operating at a slightly higher temperature of 1200°C to give a uniform consistency, that is, the various layers of glass allowed to become a homogeneous mass at a uniform temperature. It is then blown to the required size and shape whilst being turned continuously. In some cases the finished object is made up of several such blown pieces.

When the piece is finished it is placed in an annealing cabinet maintained at 450°C. At the end of a day's work this is then left for 72 hours during which time the temperature is progressively reduced to room temperature.

Joseph Nuttgens
Stained Glass Window Artist

Joseph Nuttgens studied at the Central School of Art and the Royal College of Art. After a period of teaching he worked for Patrick Reyntiens and John Piper before taking over his father's studio in 1982. The studio is located deep in the Chilterns countryside near High Wycombe, very close to where Eric Gill had his studio in the 1920's. Joseph has undertaken many commissions including the Benjamin Britten Memorial Window in Farnborough, to John Piper's design; the Tyneside Industrial Heritage window in St Mary's Cathedral in Newcastle-on-Tyne and the Millennium Window in Durham Cathedral. He designed and made the Fire Restoration Window in the Royal Private Chapel in Windsor Castle to replace the one lost in the fire of 1992, with some panels depicting the chaos of rescuing priceless artefacts and firemen fighting the blaze. For the same chapel, he designed two small side lights commemorating the Royal Golden Wedding. He has also designed and made numerous works for schools, offices and private customers as well as carrying out extensive renovations. At the time this photograph was taken he was working on a church memorial window. He is a Fellow of the British Society of Master Glass Painters

Strictly speaking, only glass to which paint and stain have been applied should be called stained glass. This process is always fairly expensive; panels made from unpainted coloured glass are more often referred to as 'Architectural Glass'. As an artist, Joseph aims to create windows which survive the test of architecture and which are sympathetic to situation and history, whether in a new building or medieval church, and are appropriate to the light and atmosphere of the building. Stained glass can provide a focal point or create a discreet interior light. The design of stained glass must be given priority, but the technical standards for stained glass, both for ancient and new buildings, are very high so the main part of the studio is concerned with glass cutting, firing, etching and glazing.

Stained glass can be fitted into ancient stonework, new wood or metal frames or into double glazed units and his studio employs a skilled specialist for this part of the work. Joseph's work has been featured on BBC and most independent TV channels as well as in national newspapers, trade, craft and lifestyle magazines. The Windsor windows were illustrated in Adam Nicholson's book *Windsor Restored*, recording the renovations after the fire at Windsor Castle

Ronald Pennell - Glass Engraver

Ronald Pennell is arguably the most influential engraver of glass in the country and is probably the only artist to create his own sculptures in glass which he then engraves. He is highly acclaimed worldwide, and has engravings in numerous collections in America, Europe and Japan including the Museum of Modern Art Hokkaido, the Museum of Applied Arts Prague and the Victoria and Albert Museum in London. He has had numerous solo exhibitions and recordings of his life and work forming a Pennell Archive have been made for The National Story Collection at the British Library.

On leaving art school in 1955 Ronald won a major scholarship to study gem engraving in Germany and on his return to England was offered a lectureship at Birmingham College of Art where he taught metal engraving and design. However, it was not long before he realised that, as a teacher, he would inevitably suffer a loss of technique due to the demands of lecturing and demonstrating rather than practising. Luckily his wife, who also taught at the college, felt the same way so in 1964 they moved to Herefordshire where they now have an idyllic cottage and garden studios overlooking the River Wye. He spent the next ten years specialising in rock crystal engraving, a skill which has a great history and which led to the development of glass engraving by the Bohemian Master, Caspar Lehmann in the 17th century. In 1974 John Houston, who was then exhibitions officer at the newly formed Crafts Council, saw his work and offered him the first solo exhibition at the Crafts Council Gallery. The exhibition 'Ronald Pennell: Rock Crystal Engravings' subsequently toured the country. Shortly afterwards, seeking a new challenge, he engraved his first pieces on glass using the same gem engraving lathe with diamond cutting wheels. His experience of the much harder rock crystal engraving allowed him to work with greater freedom. Whilst some glass engravers use a hand-held rotary diamond cutter, Ronald chooses to use a wheel engraving lathe and moves the glass to its diamond wheels to achieve his unique engravings. Being a natural sculptor Ronald is able to think three dimensionally when engraving his images spontaneously without reference to drawings.

Entering his works into 'New Glass 79', an international exhibition of World Glass at The Corning Museum of Glass, New York, he was one of only two engravers selected. Ronald's work was given a unanimous jury vote and its successful international reception quickly established him as one of the most significant engravers of the modern glass movement.

In 1993 he was made an Honorary Professor at the Academy of Applied Arts in Prague and awarded the Medal of Honour in recognition of his outstanding contribution to the Academy. In 2000, *Modern Myths: the Art of Ronald Pennell* was published to accompany a major retrospective exhibition. After several years as a visiting professor at the University of Wolverhampton he was awarded the title of Honorary Professor of Glass in 2001.

Norman Ackroyd
Etcher and Engraver

Norman Ackroyd studied at Leeds College of Art and subsequently at the Royal College of Art, London. He was elected a Royal Academician in 1991 and made Senior Fellow, Royal College of Art, in 2000. He has had solo exhibitions both in Britain and abroad and has prints in many galleries including The Tate, the British Museum, Museum of Modern Art in New York, plus numerous embassies and national galleries around the world. He has produced many books illustrating his art, the most recent being *A Line in the Water* in collaboration with Douglas Dunn who wrote the poetry. Norman regularly produces boxed sets of etchings; the latest entitled *St. Kilda Revisited*. He travels regularly in search of new locations within Great Britain and Ireland. The pull of coastal areas is strong; there is very little of the western coast of Eire he has not painted or etched at some time over the last several decades.

Printmaking involves the transfer of ink from a prepared metal plate to paper by means of a press. The copper, zinc or steel plate is first coated with wax. Using a variety of tools, the lines of the picture are drawn by scraping away the wax and exposing the metal. On immersion in an acid bath the acid reacts with the exposed metal to create microscopic grooves. If continuous tones are required, such as for sky or clouds, an aquatint can then be applied to create a suitable surface to retain the ink. In this process, a fine resin powder is deposited onto the plate which is then heated (see main photograph) to fuse the grains of powder onto the metal, thus creating a matrix of microscopic resin dots. On re-immersion into the acid bath the spaces between the dots become etched. The resin is then removed with methylated spirits before proceeding further. At this point a trial print is made, by rubbing printers ink over the grooves of the plate. After removing excess ink the plate is placed onto dampened paper and rolled through the press where the pressure applied causes the paper to be forced into the grooves and ink to be transferred. This proof print is then examined, and further etching and aquatinting carried out if required until the final image is deemed to be finished. The plate is then electroplated with 2 microns of steel at which point it is ready to make the first print of the edition.

To achieve a quality print requires the press to be absolutely rigid - hence the huge weight of these cast iron machines. Norman has two presses; the larger, built around 1900, weighs three tons and has supports built up from the cellar floor below. He produces editions of 90 for sale, plus a further 9 artist's proofs. After the last print of an edition has been made the plate is cancelled.

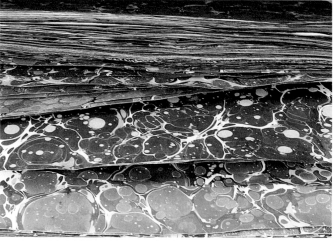

Katherine Brett
Marbled Paper Maker

While at college in 1980 learning bookbinding, Katherine was introduced to marbled paper and thought it would be fun to make. It was not directly part of her course, but she read books and learnt the craft although it took her a long time to master the technique of making the paint float. However, master it she did and she started selling small sheets of marbled paper to friends. In due course she was asked by Falkiner Fine Papers of London if she could make larger sizes and thus commenced the production of 20 inch by 30 inch sheets of hand-made marbled paper which she now sells worldwide.

Its origins are obscure, but paper was marbled in Japan as early as the twelfth century. The technique had spread to Persia by the fifteenth century, to Turkey by the seventeenth century and was being manufactured in Western Europe by about 1630.

Paper marbling is a method of transferring onto paper a fluid design which is similar to the patterns found on marble, hence the name. There are various methods for marbling paper, the traditional method uses carrageenan (an extract of seaweed) to make a gelatinous solution on which water based paints are floated. With the final pattern in mind, paint is dropped, or spattered, onto the gel; one colour at a time, until a fairly dense pattern of several colours floats on the surface. The design is then created using a variety of techniques. For the nonpareil pattern similar to that reproduced as end papers for this book, a thin rod is pulled through the surface and moved from side to side whilst steadily progressing along the length of the trough. Then, a comb (a piece of wood with closely spaced pins), is dipped into the surface and steadily drawn down the trough creating a further pattern variation. Various differing combs can be used to create other patterns such as 'Peacock', 'Wave' or 'French Curl'. Alternative patterns can be created by adding caustic elements to the paint such as potassium carbonate or turpentine to create traditional designs such as 'Tigers eye' or 'Stormont'. Once the desired pattern is floating on the gel, the paper, which has been pre-treated with a mordant, is carefully laid over the surface causing the paint to adhere; it is then drawn from the trough and hung up to dry. Any residual paint is removed from the surface of the gel and the whole process repeated.

Katherine specialises in reproducing historic designs, producing traditional hand-marbled papers for the bookbinding trade. The most commonly used pattern is called 'Old Dutch' which originated in the seventeenth century. In addition to those mentioned above, others popular at the time included 'French Shell' and 'Gloster'. Nonpareil patterns remained popular throughout the Victorian era. Traditional papers were often highly polished with beeswax before use which enhanced the colour, making them more durable. Even with the most careful repetition of paint deposition, no two hand-made papers can ever be quite the same; that is their beauty.

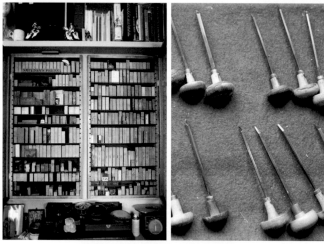

Simon Brett - Wood Engraver

Simon Brett learned wood engraving from Clifford Webb at Saint Martin's School of Art, London, where he studied principally as a painter. As a painter he travelled to Mexico, Denmark and France before returning in 1971 to teach at Marlborough College Art School. In 1989 he left the College and became self-employed as a full time engraver working mainly to commission. He has created engravings for many works including *The Reader's Digest Bible* and numerous books for the Folio Society. The second revised edition of his own book *Wood Engraving - How to do it* was published in 2000 and in the same year he published *An Engraver's Globe*, a survey of wood engraving world-wide. In 2009 his work was included in the book *A Being More Intense* which featured the art of six past chairmen of the Society of Wood Engravers. Simon is a Fellow of the Royal Society of Painter-Printmakers and was chairman of The Society of Wood-Engravers from 1986 until 1991.

Simon works from his studio in Marlborough which also houses his impressive library of books. During my visit he was working on a fine print book *Pericles, Prince of Tyre*. He was arranging the layout of the book and had made a mock-up in which he had pasted copies of his drawings and illustrations that he would later use as the basis for creating the wood engravings. As each batch of engravings was completed it was being sent to Simon's collaborators, Crispin and Jan Elsted at their Barbarian Press in British Columbia, where they had designed the typography and were printing the pages of the book

The reason for making a wood engraving is to make a print for a book illustration or a limited edition. An engraver uses the end grain of the wood to enable the cut to be made in any direction and to ensure that the block renders fine detail. The 'burin' is the generic term for all engravers' tools. There are four main types of tool - the graver, spitsticker, the tint tool and the scorper - each made in different sizes and each producing a different type of cut. It is the width of cut, rather than its depth, that is significant and they are made such that their handles and their length allow the tool to become an extension of the artist's hand.

The block is covered with a coating of black writing ink onto which the image is drawn. The cuts are made where light areas are required on the finished print, noting that the finished image will be laterally inverted. The block is then positioned; paper is placed on top, the assembly slid into the press and pressure applied such that the image is transferred from the top surface of the block onto the paper. Simon has two presses - one made in 1869 and a larger one from 1854; such presses are no longer manufactured, those which do exist are traded amongst engravers.

Nicky Clacy - Papier-Mâché Artist

Nicky works for the Tourist Information Centre in Beverley, Yorkshire and was asked if she could make a Christmas window display, but without any funds being available. Using very basic materials she decided to create a papier-mâché display; on completion it attracted great local interest. Nicky has no formal training in art but, although claiming not to be good at drawing, from childhood she has always modelled things in plasticine and clay. She has an eye for detail and proportion.

Inspired by a sculpture in the gardens at Burton Agnes she then made an elephant, soon to be followed by a zebra head and a giraffe head - the idea being that animal heads on spikes would make an interesting garden display amongst the foliage. She was later invited to enter the Beverley Open Art Exhibition for which she modelled full sized figures. She is also a regular exhibitor at the Ferens Art Gallery in Hull as well as various other galleries throughout Yorkshire.

Nicky works to commission and has made models ranging from a small figure of a legendary 1878 Aston Villa footballer Archie Hunter for a display, to producing six head masks for the 2010 TV programme 'Big Brother'. She is a regular demonstrator at the National Garden Scheme 'Art in the Garden' where she makes models inspired by her surroundings, such as urns, statues and flowers.

There are a number of ways to make a papier-mâché model, differing in how the covering is applied. Nicky usually makes the basic framework (armature) out of chicken wire, but cardboard or even balloons may also be used. The wire netting armature is covered with strips of newspaper and brushed with glue (usually wallpaper paste or PVA adhesive) and allowed to dry. Because the ink on newspapers adversely affects the final painting, she then applies a second layer of the (much cleaner) toilet tissue as a pulp. To make the pulp, the tissue is soaked and the water squeezed out. The mass is placed in a mixer and shredded. On drying, the pulp is brittle - it is cut into small pieces, placed in a coffee grinder and ground to a powder. The resultant mass has a texture like cotton wool and is mixed with adhesive before being applied to the armature using a pallet knife.

The model is allowed to dry for at least two weeks before it is painted, using either emulsion paint or whatever paint is suitable to the environment in which it will be placed.

Joan Cutts - Egg Crafter

Forty years ago Joan read an article about Fabergé eggs which were first produced in 1885, made from precious metals, and regarded as the masterpiece of the jeweller's art. She thought it would be interesting to make similar eggs containing 'surprises', although hers would be made from real eggs. Joan does not claim to be particularly artistic, but believes the key requirements are being reasonably practical and having a lot of patience; her occupation as a nurse has prepared her well. In 1978 she wrote an article for the magazine *Gem Craft* which ended with a request that anyone who was interested in this new craft should contact her. She received more than 200 responses which prompted her, in 1979, to form The Egg Crafters Guild of Great Britain. This now has members world wide, produces a magazine, holds conferences and organises exhibitions. Joan is editor of the magazine and life President of the Guild. In 2000 she received an MBE for Services to Egg Crafting.

These decorative eggs can be made using any egg with the exception of those from wild birds and protected species such as swans. Thus eggs from pigeon, hen, duck, goose, rhea, emu and ostrich are commonly used; all are bred in captivity.

The eggs can be bought ready blown, or the contents can be removed by boring a hole at each end and blowing. The egg is then cut, either in the vertical or horizontal plane according to the design required. First, a pencil line is drawn using a rubber band around the egg as a guide. A partial groove is made using a hacksaw, followed by several further saw-cuts until the egg has been fully divided; a delicate operation. A small hinge is glued into place and a corresponding clasp on the other side. The egg is then decorated either by painting or by sticking appropriate decoration on both the inner and outer surfaces. Objects are usually placed inside the egg - for example, a miniature table set for dinner, a clock, a light, maybe even another smaller egg which can rotate; the possibilities are endless. Finally, the egg is placed on a stand, itself often highly decorated. Sometimes Joan will cut an intricate pattern into the shell; for such exacting work she uses an air operated dentist drill rotating at 480,000rpm. At that speed the instrument is vibration free and very delicate cuts can be made.

As a result of these activities, Joan became a good friend of Theo Fabergé, the grandson of the legendary man. Although the name of Fabergé was bought by a company who market luxury cosmetics, descendents of Theo Fabergé now make the eggs under the name 'The St Petersburg Collection'.

Chris Drury - Artist

Chris studied sculpture at Camberwell School of Art in London, and began a career as a figurative sculptor. However, walking through the Canadian Rockies in the 1970s with the artist Hamish Fulton made him realise that he wanted to find other ways of expressing the relationship we have with the world. Since that time, all his work has evolved through a deep experience of nature, gained by walking in some of the most remote places on earth. He has also explored other ways of seeing the world by collaborating with scientists, doctors, architects, astronomers and ecologists.

Within this study of different disciplines Chris seeks to make connections between nature and culture, inner and outer, microcosm and macrocosm. In order to be free to do this he abandons fixed style and technique, instead using whatever means and materials are needed to explore these connections. For example, his work with doctors, looking at systems in the body in relation to systems on the planet, resulted in small echocardiogram works on paper, as well as a large earth work of planted reeds and water. Wherever necessary, he works with others who have skills and expertise he says he "can never hope to match" and such collaborations have led to video and film sequences and work requiring large machinery.

Chris acknowledges a strong desire to become involved in the intimate processes of "making things with the hand and body". Most of the works that he makes involve a repetitive process using his hands, be it weaving a basket or vessel, a 70 foot high architectural structure using long green sticks or stringing 6000 pieces of dried mushroom on nylon thread to create the shape of a mushroom cloud. The long and often arduous repetitive processes involved are, he says, "hypnotic and totally absorbing".

Chris's latest exhibition, pictured here at Lochmaddy, North Uist, uses a variety of skills and crafts: it includes a woven canoe made from heather, willow and salmon skins, drawings, a stencilled gene sequence in peat, satellite imagery and digitally-produced images made entirely of densely-typed words. A twenty minute walk away is his work 'Hut of the Shadows' made in 1997. It is a dry stone and turf-roofed circular building on a promontory overlooking the Bay of Lochmaddy which echoes the shapes of the islands around it. A curved passageway leads into the dark interior, where the ghostly image of the surrounding sea and islands is projected via mirrors and a lens on to a large white rock. Chris has made fifteen of these meditative 'cloud chambers', which work like camera obscuras, and use local materials appropriate to time and place. They are in a variety of locations, from Kielder Reservoir in Northumberland to a remote forest in Kochi Province, Japan. All the work pays homage to a lifetime of travelling and walking in remote locations.

The icy wastes of Antarctica; the Himalayas, the deserts of Nevada, the rain forests of Sri Lanka and the time spent in cities, urban spaces, learning institutions, research laboratories and medical operating theatres - all of this he sees as part of "understanding our place in the universe".

Hugh Dunford Wood
Maker of Handmade Wallpaper

Hugh Dunford Wood is an artist-designer, trained at the Ruskin School of Fine Art, Oxford in the early 1970s. He was apprenticed for three years to the designer Peggy Angus in Camden Studios. It was from her that he learnt the craft of hand-made wallpaper making. Hugh's work includes painting portraits, landscapes, murals and engraving on wood, metal and glass. In the 1980's he also ran a thriving business in hand painted ties, cummerbunds and waistcoats. He has been Artist in Residence on three occasions; in 1989 with the Royal Shakespeare Company, in 2000 at the Globe Theatre in London and in 2009 at the Masterworks Foundation, Bermuda.

Hugh has been hand printing wallpaper for his own delight for decades as a background to his paintings, but public interest resulted in the creation of his handmade wallpaper business and occasional design courses in Dorset. From the moment I knocked on the door of his house in Lyme Regis it was clear this was an artist's home. For Hugh, decorating a house means applying his art - his colourful paintings adorn every wall, and each room is papered with one of his original handmade designs. He believes that art should be a celebration of life. Although to some the term 'wallpaper' means a background colour or happening, Hugh feels strongly it should be an active decorative element adding character to a room. He finds machine-made paper comparatively 'lifeless' and seeks to reinvigorate walls with his designs, which reveal the marks of their maker.

Hugh's wallpapers are block-printed, the original method of printing dating back centuries. Traditionally, blocks were carved from wood but in the 20th century, artists, including Peggy Angus, began using linoleum. The wallpaper blocks are typically 50-100cm long by 28-56cm in width. Hugh's designs are often based on studies from nature. He believes that the natural world is the greatest designer. He has a stock of over a dozen designs and creates custom blocks for clients - in one instance he created a design incorporating the flowers used in a bride's trousseau. The use of only two colours for each wallpaper gives a look which can transform each design from subtle and delicate, or warm and inviting, to one that's strikingly bold - clients can choose any two colours they like. At first a colourwash is applied by brush over the entire roll and allowed to dry. The block is then painted with the second colour which is then pressed onto the paper with a hand held roller. Each print is registered by eye. One recognises this handmade wallpaper by the unusual, mottled look of the design. This irregular texture is distinct from the uniform flatness of silk screen or machine printed wallpapers. The result is that a room gains the presence of this very human touch, offering a unique complement to paintings and furniture, in which the eye's delight will unconsciously play over the surface of these rich wall coverings.

Chris Elmer - Wood Sculptor

Chris learned his craft at the London College of Furniture and was taught by the foreman of Mallet Antiques of Bond Street. Whilst the restoration of antique furniture remains his main business, he is building up an impressive collection of contemporary wood sculptures. He uses many different woods, including lime, sycamore, mulberry and unusually, laburnum.

He has an interest in symbolism and this is evident in his carvings which incorporate a cocktail of his many skills. Chris gets his inspiration from nature - his forms have been likened to single algae cells. He feels that images of fundamental elements of nature such as pollen and plankton as seen under the electron microscope, provide infinite inspiration for three-dimensional art. At a recent London exhibition he observed that visitors who had a medical or botanical background were enthralled with his work, even likening one piece to the swine-flu virus! His carvings are eye-catching, thought-provoking and certainly make a powerful statement.

Most of the wood he uses is kiln dried - it is harder than green wood but is more stable and less likely to crack. Sometimes people bring him unseasoned wood, whole trees or pruned limbs, which he air dries over a period of time. In general it requires about a year per inch of thickness of wood before he can begin his work.

The process of carving has to take into account the direction of grain and the coloration of the wood, and he prefers to work on his creations continuously because, as he says, "one gets into a creative flow and just wants to keep carving". A large sculptural piece such as the one shown in the main photograph takes about 250 hours to complete.

Chris lives and works in a small village in the heart of the Cotswolds. When I visited, on a bright winter's morning, I found him in his workshop, a stone outbuilding by the roadside. Some of the corrugated iron roof has been replaced by transparent material for good natural lighting, the remaining parts being heavily insulated against the weather. It is a friendly and warm place and it is easy to see how, in this quiet environment, Chris can let his artistic talents flow through chisel and mallet.

Tom Hare - Willow Artist

At Art College, Tom studied 3-D design and specialised in ceramics. He set up his studio and for some years designed and made ceramic vessels. By chance he saw a magazine featuring a list of courses run by the Field Studies Council; the one on rustic furniture-making caught his attention. He enrolled and made an armchair. He was particularly impressed by the way green wood could be used without prior seasoning; he liked the short time-scale which was very different from ceramics where several firings in the furnace were required over a long period. He bought some books on basketry and, using saplings from the hedgerow, started making sculptures. He soon discovered the attraction of scaling them up and found the results fascinating.

In due course he worked at North Warwickshire College delivering an art based enrichment programme to the students, then at Harcourt Arboretum running one-day courses in basket weaving. He also enlisted the help of the National Congress of Botanical Education staff in the construction of a giant woven snake. In 2006 he worked at Kew Gardens as a workshop artist during which time they were planning their 250th anniversary celebration and also the 10th anniversary of the Millennium Seed Bank. They suggested that a display of giant seed pods would be appropriate and asked Tom to submit ideas. The display was opened in 2009 and contains eleven giant sculptures depicting a variety of seeds including a horse chestnut, a lotus seed head, poppies and sycamore seeds. They are woven out of willow and are up to 5m high. These stunning objects are located on either side of the Broadwalk on entering through the Main Gate of the gardens.

Tom uses greenwood, specifically willow, to create large woven sculptures to commission. His technique is to design a steel armature which is constructed locally and upon which he weaves the willow using a variety of different designs and sometimes colours. He uses willow from Somerset which is cut in the winter when the sap is dormant. It is left to dry and then boiled in water which gives it a rich colour. Before use it is soaked for a few days. Tom particularly favours the species 'Flanders Red'.

He teaches basketry, willow furniture making and contemporary willow work in both educational and community establishments. He has permanent exhibits at the Royal Horticultural Society Garden at Wisley, at Westonbirt Arboretum, and frequently creates sculptures for the Chelsea Flower Show and for the BBC's Gardener's World programme.

In 2010 Tom was commissioned to make three 7.5m fantasy trees for the Bellagio conservatory in Las Vegas for their autumn display.

Donald Jackson - Artist Calligrapher

Donald Jackson gained a scholarship to the Bolton School of Art at the age of 13 from whence he specialised in graphic design and calligraphy at the Central School of Arts and Crafts and City and Guilds of London School of Art. He studied at Goldsmiths College in London before teaching at Camberwell College of Art. During this time he became, and still is, the senior scribe and illuminator to the Crown Office, producing a wide variety of ceremonial documents and royal charters. He is the author of *The Story of Writing* and has contributed to various publications. He also co-produced and presented the 5 part documentary series *Alphabet: The Story of Writing*. He is currently the Artistic Director of the Saint John's Bible project based on the creation of the first hand written and illuminated bible on this scale since the invention of the printing press over 500 years ago.

He is well known internationally as a leading contemporary scribe and illuminator, having lectured at numerous universities and calligraphy and graphic arts conventions. In 1995 Donald suggested the creation of a new handwritten bible to Saint John's Benedictine Abbey and University in Minnesota as a way of celebrating the new millennium. In due course, and much to his welcome surprise, the bible was commissioned. At his spacious scriptorium in rural Wales he created most of the interpretive illuminations and, together with a small team of artist calligraphers, was responsible for hand-writing the entire text of the Old and New Testaments onto vellum using goose-quill pens. There is only one copy of the hand-made manuscript bible, arranged in seven volumes. He is also art directing the production of 360 finely printed facsimile sets using the latest technology with specially developed foiling techniques. Set number one has already been presented to the Pope; 299 others will be for sale. The entire project will have taken more than 14 years.

Donald explained how the script was specially developed for this bible and how the illuminations were created to illustrate the fascinating stories. Once the style and size of each letter has been formed it is digitised and used to create a computer generated image of each page - an intermediate procedure used to ensure each page layout contains exactly the required number of words and correct spacings. The pages are printed out full size and act as an aid to the calligraphers who handwrite each line onto vellum using a goose quill pen. Every chosen passage of the bible is read and re-read whilst Donald notes the significance of the action or drama it contains. He can then begin to build up a picture in his mind. Theological values are explored with the Monastery before and after this process and agreement is reached on how to proceed. Whilst his art illustrates the ancient past, his interpretation is very modern to reflect the world as it is today. Every mark, every detail has significance - from lines which are taken from electronically generated images of acoustic traces of hymns being sung by the monks of Saint John's, to faces which reflect the moods and characters of ancient kings and queens. This is, as Donald says, the "Dream project of a lifetime for a calligrapher".

Graham Jones - Tree Carver

Graham studied sculpture at Winchester School of Art working with a variety of materials including steel. He describes how he "felt frustrated with the seemingly two-dimensional nature of manufactured materials" and sought something with a more solid mass to inspire him. When a visiting tutor, Lee Grandjean, who is now a senior lecturer at the Royal College of Art, encouraged him to consider carving, he found that working with a piece of wood, or tree suited him perfectly, as it provided a much more interesting starting point. His future course was set. He gained his degree in 1982, and, leaving the relative security of the college, he needed somewhere to work. He spent £100 on some carving tools, walked into the woods and started carving any wood he could find that was fallen or dead. He has never stopped.

He taught wood carving for four years at the Midlands Art Centre in Birmingham. In due course he was commissioned by the Landscape Practice Group, part of Birmingham City Council, to carve trees in the city's parks as part of their project to rejuvenate the area. He now has carvings in most of the city parks. Both living and dead trees can be carved. In the case of living trees, new shoots may sprout after the carving is complete, which can lead to some interesting effects. He works primarily in the Midlands although he has carved trees elsewhere, a notable example being at New Lodge in Berkshire where he transformed an old oak into a truly eye-catching and imaginative sculpture.

His tools range from sizeable chain saws to small gauges (chisels). He frequently carves on site, that is, from a ladder or scaffolding up a tree, although more portable pieces of wood are carved at the studio. During my visit he was working on a particularly large and detailed sculpture commissioned by Dudley Metropolitan Borough Council to celebrate the exploits of Prince Rupert, cousin of Charles l, who sought refuge by hiding in a well in the grounds of Wollescote Hall in Dudley during the Civil War. Steve Field, the Dudley Borough Artist carried out the research and produced the concept design drawings from which Graham worked. The finished sculpture was installed in July 2010. It was carved from a single piece of sweet chestnut, 14ft high, up to 7 ft in diameter and weighing 8 tonnes. The project was jointly funded by Dudley MBC Liveability Project, the Friends of Stevens Park Wollescote and the Arts Council.

Graham mainly carves oak, but other woods including sweet chestnut, cedar, scots pine and more recently giant redwood have been used, all of these woods having a high tannin content. Tannin is a naturally occurring polyphenol chemical which reacts with protein to produce a substance that prevents rotting. It is found in large quantities in oak, sweet chestnut and sequoia redwood in particular. Graham's smaller wood sculptures are normally sold through galleries, but others intended for permanent outdoor decoration are always commissioned and always with close collaboration between artist and client.

Terry King - Photographer

Terry's love of photography began at the age of twelve. He acquired his first camera and "took lots of photographs of the Festival of Britain" but his parents insisted that he should continue his studies so that he could get a 'proper job'. He joined the Civil Service in the early seventies but the pull of photography was always present. Having attended a talk on the gum bichromate process, he felt that this could offer a route into photography as a career. He became obsessed with this, and his success led him to decide to leave the security of the Civil Service and become a self-employed photographer and teacher. In due course he was asked to run a year-long course at Richmond College which he called 'From Wedgewood to Bromoil', covering the different methods of making photographs since its beginning, starting with the methods used by Wedgwood to transfer images onto pottery. His philosophy is that each process, even though superseded by something more efficient, has elements that are worth preserving in terms of picture making. He now runs courses on specific processes; Platinum, Gum Bichromate, Bromoil, Gravure, Salt, Cyanotype and Albumen. Sometimes experiments lead to amendments to old processes that improves their ability to make pictures; examples include Herschel's chrysotype (gold) and cyanotype (blue). Terry's versions are known as the chrysotype rex and the cyanotype rex.

The common element in creating pictures using these processes is to first coat art paper with the appropriate chemicals, which in some cases incorporate pigments. After drying, a negative is placed onto the paper and exposed under ultra-violet light. The paper is then developed using chemicals specific to the process. Depending on the process, the paper may then be recoated and re-exposed until the desired effect is achieved. Although Terry usually uses contact negatives from his 10 x 8inch camera, he also produces contact negatives from images originating from a digital camera.

Interest in old photographic processes has increased significantly over recent years as many people become dissatisfied with the ability of digital photography to meet their creative needs. They also value the craftsmanship and aesthetic provided by alternative photography. Paradoxically, this increase in popularity is aided by the use of digital means to produce the large format negatives although the best platinum prints are still those made from negatives taken on film using large format cameras and exposed and developed for the purpose.

Terry is an internationally recognised authority on Historical Photography and Alternative Process Print making. He lectures widely both in UK and abroad. In 1997 he founded APIS (Alternative Processes International Symposium) which runs conferences in the UK and USA on alternate years. He was chairman of the Royal Photographic Society Historical Group from 2004 to 2008.

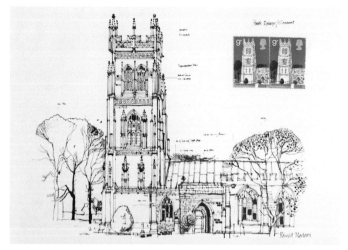

Ronald Maddox
Watercolour Painter

From early in his life Ronald wanted to be an artist. He comes from a family background of craftsmen - on one side a link with lettering and gilding, and on the other side, silversmiths. Always drawing and painting in watercolour, at the age of fourteen, as a scout, he was one of the winners of a national poster competition 'Youth Looks at Britain', sponsored by the British Travel Association. Following school he trained in Hertfordshire at the St Albans School of Art, which became the Hertfordshire College of Art and Design where, later in his career, he became a Governor and Member of the Design Committee, and where drawing and painting were encouraged.

During National Service in the RAF, after initial training he was posted to the Air Ministry Design Unit in London, working as an artist/designer on many recruiting projects for the services. During this time he was able to continue his training in illustration, design and printmaking at London Art Colleges.

He continued to paint and started to show his pictures in London exhibitions, including the Royal Institute of Painters in Water Colours. In 1959 he was elected a member of the R I. At that time he was the youngest painter to be elected since their formation in 1831. He was then elected onto the Royal Institute Council in 1962, was made Vice President in 1979 and President in 1989, a position he has held for the last 20 years. As President of the RI he is also an Honorary Member of the Royal Watercolour Society. Only the Presidents, if agreed by members of both Societies, can be a member of both organisations.

Ronald develops his painting from a real subject, first by making sketchbook drawings in pencil or small watercolour sketches, making notes to remind him of colours and other details of the location, working outside at any time of the year to get material together for a full size drawing.

Over a number of years he has worked freelance as an artist, designer and illustrator on a variety of commissions, many linked with Britain. These have included designing commemorative stamps on architectural themes, village churches, historic buildings, urban renewal, industrial archaeology, and stamps for the Isle of Man on the island's architecture. He has produced many line illustrations for telephone directories, covering many parts of the country. As a result of these commissions he has, over many years, built up a library of sketchbooks, all of which link with his work as a renowned watercolour painter.

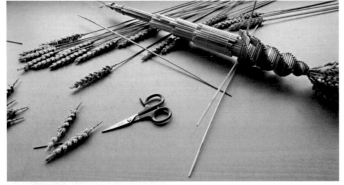

Gillian Nott - Straw Craftsman

Peering over a neighbour's fence and watching curiously at what turned out to be a straw dolly being made, proved to be the start of Gillian's long involvement with the craft. Whilst the ubiquitous straw dolly might be the public face, it is but the tip of the 'straw iceberg', the craft encompassing a wide variety of both artistic and utilitarian articles. After some initial tuition from her neighbour, Gillian acquired a book entitled *A Golden Dolly, the straw-maker's bible*, and taught herself. Whenever the opportunity arose (she was an expatriate wife spending much time abroad), she mixed with like-minded enthusiasts and soon developed her skills. On discovering the Guild of Straw Craftsmen, Gillian inevitably became involved and in due course became their Newsletter Editor and Historian, posts she still holds. Despite being self-taught she submitted her work for a qualification to The City & Guilds and not only gained the accreditation but also their Gold Medal for Excellence for that year. Gillian takes commissions, has her work in various museums and produced all the illustrations for the book *Swiss Straw Work, Techniques of a Fashion Industry*. She has also built up an impressive collection of artifacts from workers all over the world.

Whereas corn is the generic term for plants such as wheat, oats, barley and rye, the term 'straw' can also include other plants such as palms, grasses and jute, or even paper. Old fashioned long-stemmed thatching wheat straw is preferred, but with changes in farming methods resulting in wheat being bred with much shorter stems, supplies are becoming difficult to acquire. Many of the old fashioned varieties are no longer grown, indeed, the preferred species, Maris Widgeon, has been removed from the National List and so supplies are dependent on a few farmers growing from the previous year's seed - a practice which cannot continue indefinitely. Gillian has her own patch of wheat in her garden, but more out of enthusiasm rather than meeting all her needs. Newer varieties are available but so far have not found favour for very fine work. Although thatchers can use materials from different sources, they also face the same problem when making the beautiful straw finials which may be found adorning the best of the thatched roofs.

Straw is always kept damp whilst working to ensure it can be manipulated without breaking. The stem can be woven, folded or plaited into intricate shapes, or opened out and flattened, even glued together to make wider sheets from which many different shapes can be cut. Micro pieces can be cut and used for inlays; larger pieces can be cut and used for straw marquetry. Even delicate golden threads can be produced by splitting the straw down the length of its stem, and plying two of these together to produce a cord. Straw hats can be woven using beautiful designs. Straw dolls of incredible intricacy can be made, their faces being formed from modelling clay which is then covered with flat strips of straw forming the 'skin'. And of course, a very wide variety of straw dollies can be made, dollies which are still used today by many country farmers as part of the celebrations at the end of the harvest.

Bernard Middleton
Bookbinder and Restorer

Bernard Middleton MBE is one of the world's leading book restorers, having spent his whole life in the trade. Following initial craft training at the Central School of Arts & Crafts from 1938, he served his apprenticeship at the British Museum Library Bindery in 1940. In 1949 he became a Craftsman-Demonstrator at the Royal College of Art, and two years later, at the age of 27 was appointed manager of Zaehnsdorf Ltd., an internationally known firm of bookbinders, then located at Cambridge Circus. In the same year, he was elected a Fellow of the Royal Society of Arts. In 1953 he set up his own business and remains a self-employed bookbinder. Whilst he no longer accepts commissions for designed bindings, he continues to restore antiquarian books and bind them in period styles in his house in Clapham.

Meeting Bernard is a most civilised experience. I was welcomed into his study where we sat around a green baize covered table. Most of the walls of the room were covered with bookcases, as was the hall through which I was ushered. There were many more books upstairs, apparently, despite a collection of about 2000 books relating to the history and practice of bookbinding having been transferred to the Rochester Institute of Technology in New York State. Bernard has written several major books including: *A History of English Craft Bookbinding Technique* (1963/1996) and *The Restoration of Leather Bindings* (1972/2004). Also, *Recollections: A Life in Bookbinding* (2000), plus many dozens of articles and papers.

From the very early days Bernard built up what is now an international reputation for the restoration of antiquarian books which often involves the replacement of missing leaves. In such cases he locates an intact copy of the book in a major library and acquires photographs of the requisite pages. A block maker produces magnesium plates with which Bernard prints facsimiles on appropriate old paper and does any necessary ageing to match adjacent leaves in the book. He has several means of achieving this, including the use of gravy browning and dust from various parts of the bindery. One of his most important assets is a huge collection of book papers of all periods from the early 16th century. Also of great importance to him and his work are the thousands of finishing-tools which are used for gold tooling on leather and for the lettering on spines.

Having practised his craft since 1938, except for three years in the Royal Navy during WWII, Bernard's retirement is unlikely to be long delayed.

Stuart Mortimer
Artist Wood Turner

Stuart first started wood turning at school but is essentially self-taught. After a career in the police, during which time he became a proficient turner, he decided to pursue the craft professionally when he retired. He went on to win several national awards and has since built up an international reputation, being well known for his artistic approach and spiral work. He exhibits regularly in the UK and USA and sells to serious collectors, many of whom have come to realise that his work has investment potential. Not surprising therefore was his invitation to have a three week exhibition in David Linley's showroom in London in 2008. His work is bought by interior designers and he is a teacher, demonstrator and consultant to turners and turning groups throughout the U.K., Europe, Scandinavia, U.S.A. and Australia. His work is also now being acquired by museums in the USA. He does reproduction work for trade and English Heritage. He is the author of the book *Techniques of Spiral Work* and has published a video entitled *Wet Turning with a Difference*. Stuart is a Liveryman of the Worshipful Company of Turners; he is heavily involved with the Youth Training and Development Programme which began at his workshop 6 years ago. This programme is free to young turners and is sponsored by the Association of Woodturners of Great Britain and the Worshipful Company of Turners.

Stuart has an affinity with trees and their product and is continually on the look-out for unusual pieces of material. Every piece of his work is produced with meticulous care and finished to the highest standard for tactile and visual pleasure. His work is hand crafted on and off a lathe using hand-held electrical power tools as well as traditional carving tools. To make a twisted piece is time consuming. The overall shape of the article is turned on the lathe and the inside hollowed out. Then, with the lathe still turning, a series of equally spaced concentric pencil marks are made over its length. With the lathe at rest, diagonal marks are drawn between circles which then act as a guide for the next step. This step involves using a hand-held powered dremmel - a rotating arbour - with which Stuart creates a series of openings in the side of the piece. These are then meticulously sanded until the required finish is achieved. He decorates his pieces, such as twisted miniature goblets, candlesticks, bowls and boxes, using various techniques including burning, carving, ebonising, and piercing.

His major works are often easily identified by a twisted finial that has become his trademark. He is the holder of the World Record for turning the largest bowl, a record authenticated and certified by the Guinness Book of Records. The bowl, turned in the USA in 1997, is made out of a single solid piece of Sitka spruce measuring 8ft 4½ inches diameter at the outer natural edge, with the bowl at its solid centre being 7ft 9½ inches in diameter.

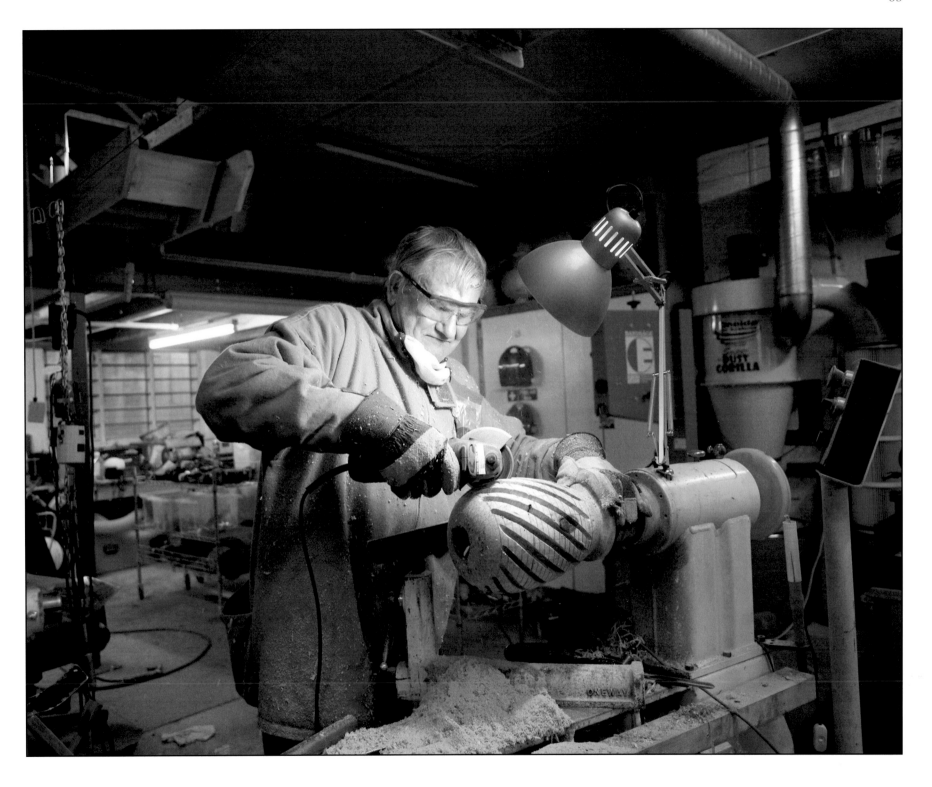

Stephen Mottram - Marionettist

With a degree in International Relations and Russian, Stephen intended to become a diplomat. But he won a scholarship to study in Sweden for a year and decided to use the opportunity to go to Art School there. Although he studied various art forms, he was surrounded by people making wood carvings and decided that his future lay in that direction. Perhaps this was not too surprising as his grandfather was a carpenter. In 1980 he went to work for Chris Somerville and Eric Bramall at the Harlequin Puppet Theatre in North Wales. In 1996, when Eric died, Chris established an annual award for excellence in the field of string puppetry, the recipient chosen by 'The British Puppet and Model Theatre Guild'. This Harlequin Award is now widely regarded as the 'Oscar of Puppet Theatre'. In 2005 Stephen was presented with this prestigious trophy.

The term 'puppet' is generic and covers all kinds of theatrical doll; a marionette specifically refers to a string-operated figure. Stephen's puppets are made from pine, each piece hand-carved, each puppet extensively jointed. His puppets have evolved over the years from being relatively large in his early days to more recent ones which are smaller and technically superior. They are, as Stephen points out, 'movement machines'. Although he is an acknowledged master in making puppets, his aim is always to create performances which cause the audience to leave the theatre talking about the theatrical content rather than the medium of puppetry.

Stephen gives regular performances in theatres both in UK and abroad. His most highly acclaimed show, 'The Seed Carriers', is a haunting piece intended for adult audiences about a race of small creatures that look remarkably like humans, but are really more like insects or plants and are harvested for their seeds. It has toured extensively and won numerous national and international awards. The show uses approximately 40 puppets, many being generically the same figures but having subtle differences to suggest ageing throughout the show or to react to different lighting. Stephen's plays have no spoken words, but have powerful electro-acoustic music, produced by Glyn Perrin. Every minute and second of the show is closely choreographed for maximum effect.

Over recent years puppet theatre has generated renewed interest with shows containing puppets being staged in West End theatres. Courses are run by the London School of Speech and Drama and at RADA. Stephen teaches puppetry at the University of Essex and The Institut International de la Marionnette in France.

Jim Patterson - Paper Maker

Jim Patterson is a fourth generation papermaker. His great grandfather, originally a shepherd, later worked in a mill at Hexham, as did his grandfather and father; Jim joined the same mill after having learnt papermaking technology at college.

In the mid 1970's Jim worked at Frogmore Mill in Hemel Hempstead, leaving in 1986 to start his own business, Two Rivers Paper, at Pit Mill in Somerset. In 2002 The Paper Trail Trust took over operations at Frogmore to save it as a heritage site and in 2006 invited Jim to return as their mill manager. However, after three years the Trust could no longer afford to run the large paper machine so he left their employment and became a tenant, making handmade paper in part of the mill and operating their small mill under licence. Now, all papermaking at Frogmore is managed by his business, Two Rivers Paper.

Jim's real passion is hand-made rag paper which he makes at both mills. Rag papers are generally made from 100% cotton, although the term is also used to include papers which have a linen content. Cotton and linen rags are torn into small pieces by hand, placed into a hollander beater and sized using a pH neutral additive. The mixture is then passed under a barred beater roll where the rags are further torn apart and beaten for four hours. The resultant fibre slurry is poured into a large vessel, approximately one metre square, where the temperature is raised to aid drainage. A mould is dipped under the surface, lifted out and rapidly moved from side to side to allow the pulp to settle. The amount of slurry on the mould is determined by the depth of the rim, or deckle. The mould is allowed to drain before being transferred to a suction table where further water is removed. The deckle is then removed and the mould turned over to release the moist paper onto a woven woollen felt - a step known as couching. From there it is placed onto a stack of previously made sheets, each separated by a cloth felt whose surface is unique to the mill. Small batches are pressed to remove further moisture before being individually hung in the room and slowly air dried under ambient conditions.

One of the major characteristics of handmade paper is that it has no 'grain', as the fibres are not aligned with any one side as they are in machine-made paper. The thickness and weight of the sheet depends on the ratio of fibre to water in the vat.

Jim usually makes two traditional English sizes of paper: 22in x 30in (Imperial) and 16in x 20in (Copy draught), although they also make Demy and Royal. Most of their production is watermarked 'Two Rivers'. They use the terms 'gallery' and 'library' to differentiate between paper made for artists and that made for fine book production, certificates and conservation.

They are the only company remaining in the UK still commercially producing hand-made paper.

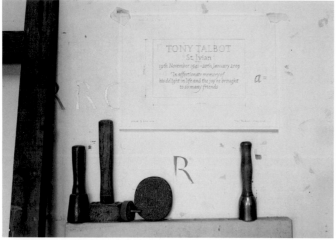

Tom Perkins
Letter Designer & Carver

Tom trained at Reigate School of Art and Design after which he worked for Richard Kindersley in London from 1976 to 1977. Thus continued an illustrious line as Richard was the son of David Kindersley who worked for the renowned Eric Gill. In 1982 Tom set up a workshop in Sutton, Cambridgeshire and, in addition to carving to commission, also taught lettering at the Roehampton Institute. He currently teaches short courses at West Dean College in Sussex, for the Memorial Arts Charity, in Cambridge and for the Prince's Foundation in London. He is a Fellow of the Royal Society of Arts, of the Temenos Academy, of the Society of Designer Craftsmen, and of The Calligraphy and Lettering Arts Society. Tom designs book jackets and has published numerous articles and, in 2007 a book, entitled *The Art of Letter Carving in Stone*. In 2009 Tom completed two plaques for Ely Cathedral, including one to celebrate 900 years of consecration; he also has examples of his work in Buckingham Palace and the British Museum.

People are often surprised to learn that anyone still hand-carves inscriptions in stone. Of course, machines are widely used for this purpose, but these use conventional typefaces which may not necessarily suit all occasions. Hand carving brings individuality to the work. An understanding of letter forms is essential, and knowledge of Roman capitals, historically the fundamental basis of the craft, is a great advantage. The basic technique of letter carving in stone uses V-incised letters, that is, letters whose cross-section is vee-shaped. The section angle is normally 90 degrees although where letters are to be carved more deeply, for example if the stone is going to be located out of doors, then an angle of 60 degrees may be used. After the letters have been drawn on the stone, the technique of chasing is used whereby the chisel is gently tapped so that it moves forwards through the stone. Other carving techniques, such as chopping (removing larger pieces of stone) or stabbing (where the chisel moves continuously forward), are used depending on the size of lettering and the amount of stone to be removed. Where relief letters are to be carved, the opposite procedure is used; a V-shaped line is first made on the outside of the letter before removing the remaining background stone.

As an accomplished calligrapher, Tom has the ability to draw any letter shapes that can be carved. Watching him work I was impressed by his meticulous approach; the gentle tapping of the chisel slowly producing beautiful lettering. He continues to develop and refine his own distinctive letterforms which are instantly recognizable by fellow carvers.

A wide variety of stone can be carved, but Tom prefers Welsh and Cumbrian slate on account of its fine structure and excellent contrast when incised. The stone has to be durable as it may be exposed to severe weather conditions and is expected to last for many years, or even centuries.

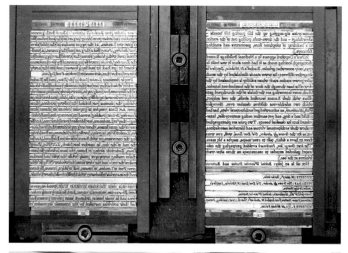

John Randle - Letterpress Printer

John's love of printing started at the age of fourteen when he was introduced to the school press at Marlborough College. From that moment, printing was all he ever wanted to do. On leaving school he trained at the London School of Printing which gave him a good technical background. He then worked for a publisher in London. In 1971 he set up his own press in an old fruit storing shed in the grounds of Whittington Court, a large country house in Gloucestershire and for three years retreated there at weekends with his wife Rosalind to pursue his hobby. In 1974 he left London and started publishing professionally. In the late seventies, desktop publishing was being introduced and by the early eighties, letterpress printing ended almost overnight. As a consequence, equipment was being scrapped and it was opportune for enthusiasts like John to acquire their equipment for virtually the price of the transport. Such was the way he obtained his 1935 Wharfedale cylinder press for £50, and later, his Heidelberg press.

The three key points in printing are the typeface, the press and the paper. The quality of paper is fundamental to making a fine print book, a feature John considers lacking in most modern books. He purchases most of his paper from Germany but in 1980 was fortunate to be able to buy 20,000 sheets of hand-made paper from the Oxford University Press, some dating back to the days of William Morris. Although some type is set by hand - each letter of each word individually placed in the composing stick - John also uses a Monotype machine whereby the operator types the text and the machine produces the text block from molten lead at a rate of one letter per second. He has several of these machines and is fortunate to have the services of a colleague who worked with them and is still able to maintain them. After the lead type has been used and the edition printed, the lead is recycled.

John publishes a variety of books, all with illustrations of one sort or another. They are bought by collectors all over the world, with over half being sold in the USA where there is a very strong following for fine press books, many institutions placing standing orders for them. The print run varies but is usually between 100 and 350. He also publishes 'Matrix', the Press' annual 'review for printers and bibliophiles'. John's books occasionally contain colour illustration in the form of multi-coloured wood-engravings or linocuts. 'Matrix' includes lithographic colour reproductions, and a more recent title includes digitally-drawn and printed colour illustration on mould-made paper. Such is the move to happily combine old and new technology.

Derek Richards - Decoy Duck Carver

Whilst living in California in the 1980's, Derek, a former London advertising photographer, discovered decoy ducks, said to be one of America's truly unique folk art forms.

On returning to England in 1985, Derek met the late Bob Ridges, a retired Master Mariner, who is credited with bringing decoy carving to the U.K. Having attended one of Bob's courses he subsequently met and worked in Virginia with Mark McNair, one of America's leading contemporary carvers. Derek is a founder member of the British Decoy and Wildfowl Carvers Association, and is also a member of the Somerset Guild of Craftsmen.

He uses only Atlantic White Cedar which he imports from America, and traditional carving tools - an axe for rough shaping and a wooden spokeshave and files for finishing. To make a duck, Derek first cuts two blanks from three inch thick planks of wood; these will become the upper and lower parts of the body. The head and neck are made from a solid piece of timber, shaped using knives. Each part of the body is hollowed out and then joined. At this point the duck is floated on water and any tendency to list is corrected by further removal of wood from the inside. The shape is completed using knives and cabinet makers' files. Next, the carving is smoothed by oiling and burning, an old American technique which Derek says gives a perfect finish without the need for too much sanding. Finally, the duck is painted using oil paints. His birds have a very individual style and have become highly collectable.

Decoying birds in this way goes back many thousands of years to the Native Americans. They used skin-covered straw ducks to decoy wildfowl to within bow and arrow range, as evidenced by decoys found in caves in Nevada which have been carbon dated. The early settlers could not use the British/Dutch method of decoying using netted tunnels, as the areas of water in America were so much larger, so they copied the Native Americans' method using wood to make the models. It is said that they would not have survived the early harsh winters had it not been for this. With the opening up of the eastern seaboard of America, from the mid 19th century until 1918 when 'market gunning' was stopped, wildfowling and hence decoy carving was big business. It employed many now famous carvers, whose birds are much sought after in the auction houses of the United States, and are known to change hands for hundreds of thousands of dollars. The modern craft, whether highly detailed or decorative, along with the more original stylized form, can be said to have originated with the publication in the early 1920's of a book entitled *Wild Fowl Decoys* by the architect Joel Barber, who first saw the intrinsic artistic value in these very practical objects.

Olwen Tarrant - Oil Painter & Sculptor

Olwen Tarrant is the only woman to have been President of the Royal Institute of Oil Painters in its proud 128-year history. At school in Newport, South Wales, she was always sketching - hands, faces, figures. Once she was drawing a rather severe teacher and discovered that the teacher was looking over her shoulder; instead of a scolding, she received high praise. She studied painting, sculpture, anatomy, printing and art history at the St John Cass School of Art and won her first prize for painting at London's Guildhall. The judge was Sir Charles Wheeler, the former president of the Royal Academy, who bought her painting for his own collection. She has won many awards, appeared on television and written articles for art magazines. She has lectured widely and her work has appeared in numerous art text books.

After submitting her work for the annual exhibition of the Royal Institute of Oil Painters (ROI), Olwen was invited to become an Associate Member. The Institute normally requires an artist to show work for a period of five years before being elected a full member; Olwen achieved this in one year in 1984. She became the first female President of the Royal Institute of Oil Painters in 2000 and was made a Fellow of the Institute at the completion of the maximum period of five years as President. She met members of the Royal Family, leading politicians, actors, academics and many others at the Mall Galleries, the prestigious home of the ROI near Trafalgar Square.

In England, Olwen paints mostly in her studio overlooking the Malvern Hills. She frequently starts a new canvas in the studio, having only the initial element of an idea in her mind. As the painting progresses, figures or objects appear, colours and shapes present themselves until the final picture emerges. She often paints figures from memory, aiming to show on canvas the feeling of pleasure she has when viewing a situation or a landscape and loving the inter-relationship between people and colours. Olwen paints her subjects as she perceives them, rather than trying to produce an accurate reproduction of the scene. She spends a considerable time each year painting on site on the Spanish mainland or in the north of Mallorca.

She carries her easel, canvas and paints round the Mallorcan villages, soaking up the atmosphere where everyday life meanders on at its own pace. Olwen speaks Spanish and is able to talk to people about their lives and about her work. They invite her into their homes and offer to let her leave her easel and paints overnight. She is sometimes surrounded by children "who ask the most intelligent and relevant questions". Nowadays she paints mostly in the mornings. At one time she relaxed (using the term loosely, she says) by horse riding and sailing in her own yacht in the Mediterranean. Nowadays it is walking over the chameleon mountains, gently undulating hills and along the Mediterranean coast, finding tucked-away restaurants where they serve paella and the most inventive menus of the day.

Christine Palmer

Aasha Tyrrell - Gilder

Aasha graduated in Art History and Archaeology at Bristol University, following which she obtained a Diploma in Conservation at the City & Guilds of London Art School. In 1979 she jointly founded the company 'Carvers & Gilders', originally with three other partners, of whom only Christine Palmer now remains as joint owner. Christine graduated in Fine Art at Maidstone College of Art and completed a post graduate course in restoration at the City & Guilds School of Art where they all met. The company is a conservation and restoration practice specialising in fine woodcarving and gilding. The majority of their work is in the English and European tradition, mostly dating from the late 17th Century to the mid 19th Century, but they also work with objects from all over the world and of all periods. Their clients include museums, national collections, public organisations, private collectors, interior designers, architects and individuals. They have undertaken long-term projects for Woburn Abbey, Windsor Castle, Osborne House, Harewood House, Spencer House, Houghton Hall, Hampton Court and Uppark amongst others. They are members of various professional associations, including the Master Carvers Association, and have been Royal Warrant Holders to the Queen since 1989.

There are two methods of gilding onto a prepared timber surface: water gilding and oil gilding. Aasha uses both techniques but specialises in the former, which gives a rich, highly decorative finish suitable for fine artefacts, carved furniture and mirror frames. Oil gilding, also suitable for architectural elements and exterior work, is used effectively but less frequently on fine furniture. Both gilding methods require considerable preparation before the gold is applied in order to hide the grain of the wood and provide a perfect surface that can emulate solid gold. To prepare a new piece for water gilding, between five to ten coats of gesso (a warm fluid mixture of animal size and chalk whiting) are applied to the wood to build up a thick layer. When dry, the surface is smoothed, carved forms are redefined and sometimes further decorative detail is cut in. The gesso layer is generally sealed with a wash of yellow ochre size followed by a coat of bole (an extremely fine clay) usually pink/red/brown in colour. This smooth, polished surface is then wetted and the gold leaf applied.

Gold leaf is available in various colours and purity, ranging from 24ct to 7ct. A 'regular' coloured leaf of 23.5ct is most often used and is equally suitable for exterior or interior use. The gold is beaten to a thickness of 0.1 micron (approximately 1/250,000 inch) and supplied in booklets of 25 leaves, each 80mm square. Gold leaf is thin, extremely delicate, and cannot be touched by hand. So, when gilding, Aasha places a number of the leaves onto the back of a gilding pad and then, with a gilder's tip, transfers one leaf at a time to the object, where it settles and is drawn onto the surface. Each leaf is laid with a small overlap which is softly brushed away when dry and the loose fragments of gold are removed and recycled. The gilt surface can then be enriched by burnishing to a mirror finish. New gold is often toned to modify the brightness, especially in restoration work where existing surfaces have to be matched.

Peter White - Marqueteer

Peter's interest was no doubt encouraged by his father who was a carpenter. Whilst on holiday on Capri he was fascinated by the marquetry items being sold to tourists and his curiosity was aroused. Sensing this interest, his wife secretly bought a marquetry picture kit and his Christmas activity was assured. After two or three years with similar kits he sought a club to further his knowledge and discovered The Marquetry Society. Peter joined and contributed enthusiastically, winning prizes at national exhibitions and in particular, won the Society's coveted Rosebowl award on three occasions, making him a fellow of the Society. He has been on the committee for many years and is a past President and, since 2007, the Chairman.

Although marquetry is generally considered to have begun in Florence in the 16th century, a form of the craft has been found in the tomb of Tutankhamen. Marquetry is the covering of the entire surface of a board with veneers so as to create a picture or design; if the design is geometric then the craft is called parquetry. Marquetry differs from inlay which is the practice of inserting thin pieces of wood (or other materials) into a solid wooden base.

Until the mid 20th century most marquetry was based on saw cutting techniques, necessary due to the thick nature of the veneers. The advent of veneer slicing machines, which can cut pressure steamed logs into much thinner leaves than can be cut by a saw, meant that veneers, typically between 0.6 - 0.9mm thick could also be cut with a knife. Logs are sliced in many different ways, producing a variety of figuring and markings dependent on the timber type and its characteristics. In the 1950's a new method of working came into fashion called 'window marquetry'. This required only a sharp knife, a cutting mat and a small glue pot giving the maker complete freedom to design and produce patterns of any complexity using as many veneer types as are needed. A piece of veneer selected to form the background is marked with the pattern, usually transferred by using carbon paper. One part at a time, selected areas of the pattern are then cut out to produce a shaped window. The window is positioned over the next chosen piece of veneer which can be moved around to identify the best figuring and grain direction. The inner piece of veneer is then cut using the window as a template. This piece is then stuck edge to edge inside the window using PVA glue. The work continues in this manner until the design has been completed.

The craftsman's skill is tested when very small pieces are cut - for example, the bird's legs and feet as shown in the picture. The final work is then secured to a base board, sanded and coated with several coats of a clear protective polish or lacquer.

Julian Hart - Silversmith

Julian Hart is a fourth generation silversmith of Harts of Chipping Campden, a family business established in 1902 in The Old Silk Mill in Sheep Street near the centre of the town. George Hart, a silversmith and a member of the Guild of Handicraft, taught his son Henry. He in turn taught his son David, who today runs the business with his son William and nephew Julian. Derek Elliott, the fourth member of the group, also served his apprenticeship with David.

The Guild of Handicraft, founded in 1888 by Charles Ashbee, architect and devotee of William Morris, had been in decline since the Industrial Revolution. In 1902, to improve the quality of life for his craftsmen, Charles Ashbee moved the Guild - which included around fifty jewellers, enamellers, woodcarvers, cabinetmakers, silversmiths, French polishers and bookbinders - from workshops in the East End of London to the rural town of Chipping Campden. The group, including wives and children, descended on the town making it a centre for the study of Arts and Crafts and contemporary design in the early part of the 20th century. Harts workshop is the last operating remnant of the Guild in the town.

Today Harts is a team of craftsmen specialising in the best traditions of handmade silver. They work to commission, designing and making the widest range of silverware from thimbles, cutlery, condiment sets, bowls, claret jugs, and tea and coffee services to the largest of salvers; many based on original designs. They also have wide experience of designing and making Ecclesiastical and Civic silver. It is fascinating to view the original design books and to be able to commission a piece to exactly the same design as would have been made over one hundred years ago.

To enter the workshop is to step back in time. Bills dating from the 1940's hang from the beamed ceiling, well-used tools of the trade cover every available surface. Visitors are welcomed to watch the craftsmen at work, at the same benches and with the same tools used by George Hart at the turn of the century. A guided tour is usually on offer. This is not a staged tourist attraction; it is skilled craftsmen going about their work producing exquisite silver work as their family has before them for over a century.

Bob Hobbs - Blacksmith

Bob Hobbs is a self-taught blacksmith who worked in the family metal fabrication business before deciding to become a blacksmith in the 1970's. He bought two books on the craft, one dated 1904, the other 1925, and, for the last thirty years has worked as a professional blacksmith using both traditional and modern methods. He has spent over twenty years with the Craftsmen of Wessex helping with committee work and teaching the students on a part-time basis. In 1995 he became a Freeman and a Liveryman of the Worshipful Company of Blacksmiths and was given the freedom of the City of London.

Bob was responsible for the design and most of the construction of the Frank Day Memorial trophy. The Worshipful Company of Blacksmiths awarded him their silver medal for putting Frank's likeness on the trophy as a figurine. In 2005 he was awarded the Gold Medal; the Worshipful Company's highest award and only the fifth time it has been given in over 350 years. He is the only living blacksmith to hold this honour. A quotation by one of his peers states "that which sets a gold award winner above the rest is the contribution he has made to the craft as a whole through his knowledge of the craft and its history; the imparting of that knowledge to future smiths, the promotion of the craft through shows by exhibiting, demonstrating and organising, and his total enthusiasm and commitment to the craft as a whole over a long period of time". He has been a member of both the Crafts and the Awards Committee of the Worshipful Company of Blacksmiths for over 20 years and also judges at events throughout the country. In 2010 he was a guest judge in the BBC TV series 'Craft' featuring The Blacksmith.

The principle of the craft lies in the shaping and joining of mild steel using temperature and pressure alone; heating and hammering the metal on the anvil until it fuses together, all of which requires great precision. However, in order to provide an efficient service today these skills need to be combined with the techniques of welding and flame cutting. Wrought iron has long been regarded as the traditional material worked by a blacksmith as it is highly malleable and ductile; it is thus preferred by many for decorative work. However, the greater tensile strength and lower cost of mild steel renders it more suitable for articles such as gates, railings and staircases, chairs and tables, hinges and farm implements. Wrought iron is likely to be used for items such as door-knockers, light fittings, bowls, sculptures, jewellery and other decorative articles. As a result of these diverse requirements, there are more blacksmiths working today than there were 30 years ago.

Bob makes both functional and decorative metalwork in his forge in Somerset. He also practises the technique of repoussé whereby the reverse of the metal is hammered to form a relief image in the finished piece. Bob clearly brings a high level of art to his craft.

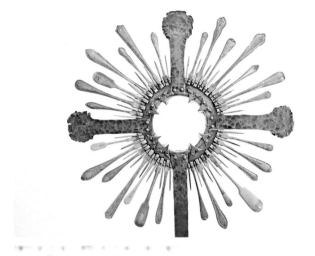

Michael Johnson - Copperworker

Michael's father worked for the British Forces Broadcasting Station and consequently the family travelled widely in North Africa and the Far East before finally settling in Australia. Watching his father make and repair sound equipment in various BFBS workshops inspired Michael to pick up scraps of copper and create little sculptures, mostly given away as presents. In Singapore, a childhood crush on the girl next door led him to her ballet classes and Michael joined in with the lessons. A career in dance was initiated, culminating many years later in the post of Artistic Director of an Australian dance company. At first, the connection between metal work and dance might seem incongruous, until one learns that Michael's overriding drive is to bring fluidity, movement and beauty to his copper work. He believes the articles he now creates are simply 'dancing with metal', making fluid and elegant shapes.

Retiring from dance at the age of 30, Michael brought to the fore the passion for metal that had never gone away. An invitation to work with his uncle, one of the worlds leading Armourers, led him back to the UK in 1994. The skills he developed in the armoury and in subsequent workshops throughout the world over the following ten years helped build his copper working skills. Living near the Cornish fishing village of Newlyn, it was hard to ignore the passion the locals had for their forbears' copper work. Newlyn is recognised throughout the world for its late 19th and early 20th century copper ware. In 1994, with endorsement from John Laity, the last in the line of the original Newlyn copper workers, Michael resurrected The Copper Works in the building where it had all started back in the 1890's.

Most of Michael's work is made to commission and he has his work displayed in a number of local galleries and at Liberty in London. He has exhibited and received commendation at the RHS Hampton Court show. He also carries out restoration work. In addition to artistic pieces, which often incorporate a range of recycled metal items, he also makes a variety of other objects, including water fountains, door handles and models of Newlyn fishing boats. Working with copper is largely a matter of hammering the metal into the desired shape using a variety of hand crafted tools, most of which Michael has made in the workshop, as did the copper workers of old. Every craftsman's tools are unique and consequently an expert eye can read the back of a beaten copper item as if it was a fingerprint, often identifying the individual craftsman. The copper is hammered into large wooden formers and Michael has a number of these to cover a range of sizes.

His workshop is in the town, close to a housing estate, where children frequently look through the open door out of curiosity. On seeing the activity several have become interested, were invited in, and shown the craft. Michael now has regular 'students' on Fridays after school or on Saturday mornings, who fashion anything from boats to a mobile phone housing! Perhaps there is nothing new here - get children interested and let them put their creativity to work.

Roy Pettitt & Brian Skilton
Raised Engravers

Raised, or relief, engraving is used to make finishing typesets and hand tools, primarily for the bookbinding trade. Roy and Brian believe they were the last apprentices to learn the skills of relief engraving from some of the finest craftsmen who themselves had worked in the trade from the 1920's. They formed P&S Engraving in 1980 and have introduced modern machinery and methods in order to remain in business, which, with their skill and eye for detail, has resulted in them supplying finishing tools to the very best bookbinders in this country and abroad. Their workshop in Portslade was originally built as a Sunday school; later used as a morgue, then various light industries until P&S Engraving took up residence.

They make many finishing tools and wheels, but the principle of their craft is to produce dies of any design, complexity and (in terms of book requirements), size. The starting point for producing a die is to draw the design on tracing paper - Roy and Brian draw these by hand, although any source of image could be used. Transferring the paper image to a one-half inch thick sheet of Perspex and using a 'spit sticker', a sharp pointed hand-tool, they scratch along each line thus making a copy by cutting a shallow groove in the Perspex. This is the master, which is usually larger than the required finished die. This is then transferred to a two-dimensional pantograph where it enables an identical, but more deeply engraved mould to be made in a block of rigid PVC to the finished size. Into this mould is poured an epoxy resin to which is added slate powder to give it suitable hard-wearing properties. This resin casting is used as the master to produce an identical relief copy machined out of brass using a three-dimensional die-sinking machine (essentially a three-dimensional pantograph). Finally a wooden tool handle is fitted. All stages require considerable skill to ensure absolute accuracy.

When used for embossing the design onto a book cover, the relief die is heated and pressed onto gold leaf which then adheres to the book material thus creating the image.

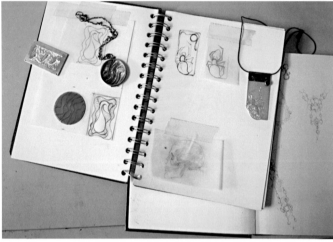

Anastasia Young - Jeweller

As a child, Anastasia loved to draw and paint, and was always "making things". After leaving school she began a pharmacology course at university but soon found it was not for her and she turned to art which was clearly her natural inclination. She completed a Foundation Course at art school during which she attended a one-afternoon course in jewellery making. This was enough to convince her to pursue this craft and start a new career, duly completing a degree at Central Saint Martins College of Art and Design in London. After a period as graduate assistant she gained a place at the Royal College of Art and obtained her MA in goldsmithing, silversmithing, metalwork and jewellery. She now teaches short courses in jewellery making at Central Saint Martins. She is the author of two technical books, *Jewellery Materials Source Book* (2008), and *The Workbench Guide to Jewelry Techniques* (2010).

Jewellery as a craft is somewhat overshadowed by mass manufactured products and components which are widely available, and whilst there is a place for this within contemporary practice, Anastasia prefers to make all her own fittings - earring hooks and brooch pins; this takes more time but increases the design integrity and value of her work. She produces pieces which frequently incorporate elements of found objects such as plastic components or small cog wheels, which are replicated into precious metals and often embellished with engraving, enamel and precious stones.

Her work has a very strong identity and it is perhaps not surprising that she tends to concentrate on one-off and exhibition pieces. Her exhibition work is intricate, unusual and frequently thought-provoking, often moving into a world of fantasy incorporating diverse objects such as bone, horn, teeth and ebony as well as small mechanical assemblies.

Her workshop is small, but there is enough space for a work bench, a hot bench and the usual drawers and storage cupboards. It comes as a surprise to learn that she shares the room with another jewellery maker who has her own work bench, though she shares the other facilities. However, it is imagination, not the working space, that produces art.

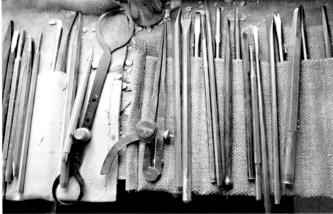

Nina Bilbey - Stone Carver

Nina's father was a master carpenter who instilled in her a strong sense of patience from an early age. She first studied ceramics at technical college, then sculpture at St Martin's School of Art in London, after which she taught art and ceramics. Although she "dabbled with stone carving" at art school, it was during a visit to Austin, Texas, where she studied at the Elizabeth Hey Sculpture Conservatory, when she was introduced to professional carvers who were able to make a living out of their craft. She was encouraged to volunteer at their workshop and spent five years travelling back and forth to the USA whilst teaching in England during term time as well as carving in the evenings. On her final return she applied to the Building Crafts College in London to study for an NVQ in masonry and an advanced City and Guilds qualification and was awarded a scholarship jointly by the Worshipful Company of Carpenters and the Worshipful Company of Masons. During this period she was awarded Student of the Year and, for services to the college, was offered admission into the Worshipful Company of Carpenters as a Freeman and given Freedom of the City of London.

From there she entered into employment and worked on such notable buildings as Hereford Cathedral, The Houses of Parliament, the Brighton Pavilion and the Grand Hotel at St Pancras Station. She also taught masonry and carving at the Building Crafts College in London. She is presently a freelance carver and also the senior carving tutor on the historic stone carving course at the London City and Guilds School of Art.

Nina is keen to point out that there is a thriving traditional hand carving industry in this country, albeit almost unnoticed by the general public. She carves historic ornament and statuary and is, as she points out, "a copy carver". The copies are taken from a model, cast, drawings or examples of surviving ornament from the building concerned. Stone is very expensive; it is often more cost effective to make the form in clay or plaster before attempting to carve; this was a method used by Henry Moore who made hundreds of small preliminary sculptures (maquettes) before attempting larger pieces.

Professional stone carvers invariably use machine tools such as grinders, air guns, drills or polishers. Whilst this might dampen the romantic image of the carver, it does allow them more time to study the form, content and balance. Some finishes would be almost impossible without the use of grinders and polishers. However, Nina always tells her students that to be really good at using machines, they have to understand and be really confident with the basic hand tools - the mallet and chisel.

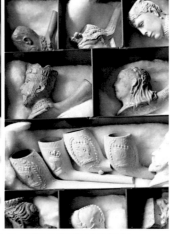

Heather Coleman - Clay Pipe Maker

In past centuries, long before municipal rubbish collections, country people would disard their household waste in nearby fields, areas which in more recent times have become interesting sites for social archaeology. As a child playing in the countryside, Heather discovered fragments of old clay pipes and became fascinated by their decoration, which including mouldings of faces. One of her favourite finds was a complete late 19th century French 'Jacob' pipe. So began her interest, and about 12 years ago her hobby became a business when she set up Dawnmist Studio to make clay pipes and other pottery artefacts. She continued to collect antique clay pipes and now has hundreds of examples, which provide inspiration for her own designs. Heather sells through the Internet and has many regular customers, including the National Clay Tobacco Pipe Archive in Liverpool which always acquires an example of each of her limited editions for their collection.

Clay pipes depicting faces of politicians, heads of state and other well-known personalities were introduced mainly by the French in the 19th century, thus inspiring other European and American makers, who incorporated faces of numerous presidents into pipes. With this in mind, and while watching the new American President taking the oath on television, Heather started her latest limited edition pipe, featuring President Obama. The first of these was sent to him as a gift. Whilst such pipes are still used by a few smokers for their original purpose, most are now bought by collectors. The decline in use of clay pipes long predates the current anti-smoking movement, having been already well under way in the late 19th Century as a result of competition from cigars, cigarettes and pipes made from more durable materials. By the time of the First World War, only a handful of makers continued this tradition which had begun in the late 16th Century when mariners returned from The New World with the first tobacco.

Heather uses slip casting, press moulding or free-form production to make her pipes. Until the late 19th century, the press moulding method was traditionally used, whereby the clay was roughly shaped, a wire then threaded through the stem to form the hole before being placed into the mould and pressed. After hand finishing and drying, the pipe was ready for firing. A more modern method, slip casting, uses a Plaster of Paris mould - often comprising several parts for complex pipes - into which is poured a clay slurry. When it solidifies, the pipe is taken out, hand finished, allowed to dry for up to 5 days, after which it is fired. Free-form production is literally sculpting or modelling a one-off pipe to commission from a block of clay before firing.

The temperature of the kiln is slowly increased to 500°C to drive off water bound to the clay and then ramped to 1050°C, firing from start to finish taking just 24 hours. After firing, the pipe may be enhanced by adding clear or coloured glazes after which it must be fired again. For economic reasons, Heather ensures that her kiln is fairly full before firing, which may involve several weeks of pipe-making. This means that the opening of the fired kiln, which I was privileged to witness, is a significant event.

Emmanuel Cooper - Potter

Emmanuel Cooper has always been interested in pottery and was fortunate to have had an inspirational art teacher at school. After studying to be a teacher he taught at art school and later at a secondary school, but after two years decided to become a potter. He initially worked for other potters whilst continuing to teach pottery part time. In due course he set up his own studio in Notting Hill before moving to Finsbury Park and then to his current premises in Primrose Hill. Emmanuel has always combined his pottery with some other activity and has continued to teach at various colleges including Middlesex University. He is currently Visiting Professor of Ceramics and Glass at the Royal College of Art and was editor of Ceramic Review until earlier this year. He has written many books on the techniques of pottery and the potters, his latest being *10,000 Years of Pottery*. He has written a definitive biography of Bernard Leach (2003), *The Potters book of glaze recipes* (2004), and *Contemporary Ceramics* (2009). His latest book, a biography of Lucie Rie, is due to be published in 2011. He is a member of the Crafts Council.

His clay is comes in plastic form, supplied by various companies in Stoke-on-Trent who deal in a wide range of stoneware and porcelain clays. Stoneware clays are used for utility vessels whilst the more refined porcelain clay is used for high quality china and art works. To prepare the clay Emmanuel adds a small amount of alumina hydrate to allow the clay to flow - to be more easily moulded and easier to handle. When I visited his studio he was working on some small vessels which he generally produces in batches of five. The only measurement he makes is to weigh the clay, these vessels each required 1lb 4oz., after which dimensions are made entirely by eye. The pot is thrown to form a hollow cylindrical shape open at both ends and, at the same time, a circular disc of clay is made which will ultimately form the base. After drying the cylinder is eased into an oval shape (see main picture), and the base attached by joining it with slip, a mixture of clay and water. Considerable care is taken to ensure a smooth outer surface to take the glaze. The base, which still retains the concentric wheel marks, is made slightly concave in order to make the pot stable. Finally the handle is formed, attached to the pot, and the whole wrapped in plastic and slowly allowed to dry. The pot is biscuit fired at 1000°C for 24 hours and allowed to cool for a further 24 hours, after which the clay is porous but strong. The glaze is applied either by dipping or pouring and the pot is then given a second firing at 1260°C for 24 hours and allowed to cool for a similar time.

Emmanuel's stoneware is characterised by his textured glazes, his porcelain by vivid reds, yellows and pale blues. Most of his work is made on the wheel, although he also hand-builds vases and other vessels using coils of clay. Examples of his work can be found in the Victoria and Albert Museum.

Sean Henry - Sculptor

Sean came to sculpture via an early interest in pottery, aged 14, preferring to make clay figures rather than pots. Following a Foundation course at Farnham Art School in Surrey in 1989 he studied for a BA in ceramics at Bristol Polytechnic. This was followed in 1990-1 by a period in California teaching with sculptor Robert Arneson at the University of California. A turning point came later in his career when, in 1998, he was awarded the Villiers-David Foundation Prize which enabled him to tour Italy. This was followed by a solo exhibition in London. Sean now exhibits regularly around the world and has many works in both private collections and public places.

Sean's inspiration originates from an observation of people. The figures usually appear pensive and preoccupied as if in a world of their own. While creating lifelike figures he is not overly concerned with making a portrait of a specific person, preferring to manipulate scale and seldom making his people life-sized; the concept of the 'golden ratio' being 1.61 times his own height is an important influence. His sculptures always retain the characteristic marks of the clay modelling process.

Having decided upon a subject, Sean takes photographs or makes sketches although occasionally a sitting will be arranged. For large scale works he uses a key-clamp system with metal rods to construct a 'skeleton' of the person - a procedure which allows him to move the 'limbs' to achieve the desired stance. This framework, or armature, is reinforced with wire before the clay is applied. The finished model is then moulded in the studio, at which point the finished mould is sent to a foundry where a bronze casting is made using the lost wax process.

The first step in that process is for Sean or the foundry to make a detailed silicone rubber mould, from which the foundry then make a wax copy for each edition of the sculpture. Once this is done, Sean returns to check the wax sculpture is exactly as he requires. The wax copy, with added runners and risers to aid the later casting process, is then coated inside and out with a ceramic material before finally being heated. At this point the wax melts and drains away giving the 'lost wax' process its name. The ceramic shell is then fired and molten bronze poured into it under tightly controlled conditions, filling the volume previously occupied by the wax. Once the sculpture has cooled and the ceramic shell removed, a long process of repair called 'chasing' begins where the various elements of the sculpture are fitted together. Sean will again return to oversee the quality of the chasing before the sculpture is cleaned by sandblasting. It is then returned to his studio to begin the process of colouring.

Sean will either paint the sculpture completely in traditional oil paints (if it is to remain indoors) or will use various types of exterior 'all weather' paints, depending on the intended final destination for the work. For his 12 metre high 'Couple in Newbiggin', Britain's first permanent offshore sculpture located almost 300m into the North Sea, he used a marine paint system designed for the hulls of ships.

Jim Keeling - Potter

While at university, his plans for a career in the law or teaching were transformed following a visit to the potter John Slade: within five minutes, Jim's mind was made up - he would become a potter. John's advice "If you can throw, you can make a living" led him to an apprenticeship at Wrecclesham Pottery in Farnham, a traditional Country Pottery now making only flowerpots. Here he learnt a centuries-old throwing technique and style. Jim founded Whichford Potteries in 1976 and moved to his current premises in 1981. Jim is hands-on; apart from running the company he also throws special pots and other vessels as well as making greater than life-sized sculptures in clay which stand majestically on the premises amid the hundreds of pots. It is company policy to provide a formal 4-5 year apprenticeship for all their throwers and his son Adam has recently completed the course. Jim is the author of *The Terracotta Gardeners* and other books on pottery. Whichford pots are sold worldwide and are particularly favoured in Japan where Jim has strong links with other potters.

The clay is brought in by the lorry load and three different clays carefully blended before being sieved, pumped into a filter press and pressed for 7-8 hours to remove excess water. At this point the clay has an uneven consistency, with a hard outer skin. It is mixed in a pugmill to homogenise it and cut into blocks. It is then covered with plastic, left for two weeks, and again homogenised. This control over the clay's consistency is considered to be of prime importance when producing high class pots with a 10 year guarantee against frost damage.

Whichford have over 250 different pots in their catalogue. For any one pot the appropriate amount of clay is weighed. The pot is thrown on a bat so that it can be removed without damage. The thrower shapes the pot and appropriate decoration is added, even a customer's coat of arms if required. At this point a date stamp is added for guarantee purposes. They make many different sizes of pots, the largest being built up from sections. These pots are thrown in two or more pieces and allowed to stiffen before being joined together. When necessary, the pots are biscuit fired before being dipped in glaze. They may then be further decorated before the final firing at over 1060°C. It is important that garden pots are not too porous such that they are attacked by frost, but still sufficiently porous to allow the plant root ball to breathe. Whichford pots achieve this critical balance.

Jim frequently displays his pots at the Chelsea Flower Show and other prestigious events. About one-third of the pots are exported to Japan with a further significant number exported elsewhere.

John Lord - Flint Knapper

John has always had a keen interest in geology and, in 1975, he and his wife Val were engaged by the Department of the Environment (now English Heritage) to take custody of Grimes Graves, a large Neolithic flint mining complex at Lyndford in Norfolk. For the next ten years they strove to master the art of flint knapping, eventually being asked to give practical demonstrations to visitors to show how the ancient flint tools were made. During this time the British Museum were conducting a five year research programme and they willingly shared their knowledge. This extensive experience led John to write a book entitled *The Nature and Subsequent Uses of Flint – The Basics of Lithic Technology*. The craft of flint knapping involves the shaping of flint to produce building materials, tools and other implements.

In 1987 John left Grimes Graves in order to pursue a career as a professional flint knapper. This led to the production of knapped flints for the building industry, and orders for a hundred tonnes or more of fist sized flints were common. John now runs courses in flint knapping at his home in Norfolk and travels throughout the country giving demonstrations at craft and country fairs.

There are two schools of knapping - the purist (as in USA) where flints are knapped only as they would have been done in historic times, and the artistic whose adherents produce similar artefacts but whose finishes are superior to those of long ago. John tends towards the latter school although is eminently qualified to make replicas of Neolithic tools. Indeed, archaeologists frequently ask him to make tools based solely on bits found on sites, that is, the actual chippings produced when Neolithic man knapped his flints thousands of years ago.

Flint forms in places where chalk deposits are found, and is created from the remains of microscopic marine creatures. A large proportion of these remains were rich in silica; over time acidic rain water percolating through the porous chalk dissolved the silica and eventually formed a build-up of pure silica, the rock we now refer to as flint.

Flint can be fractured conchoidally, that is, when hit with the appropriate tool and in the right direction, it will fracture and produce a small curved cone-shaped flake. Different sizes and shapes of hammer produce different sized flakes. The tools used range from hard pieces of flint or quartzite, to softer materials such as sandstone, through to 'soft' hammers made from wood, bone and antler. It might seem surprising that bone can be used to shape a flint, but the art lies in determining the correct orientation of the tool in relation to the edge of the flint.

Alan Spittle - Stonemason

Alan trained as a graphic designer and moved to Bath to pursue his career. Whilst there, he fulfilled a long-held ambition to own a Georgian house, albeit one which needed considerable restoration. Undaunted, he enrolled on a short course to learn the techniques of lime plastering and dry stone walling. In addition, he went on a weekend course in stone conservation and craftsmanship at Woodchester Mansion in Gloucestershire. It was as a result of this course that Alan decided to become a stone mason. After completing the work on his own house, he duly enrolled at the Building Crafts College in Stratford, London, where in 2006 he gained his stone masonry diploma. In 2009 he was the overall national winner of the Worshipful Company of Mason's Duke of Gloucester biennial Improver Masons Award, and in 2010 he was appointed a Yeoman Mason of the Company, a new award comparable to a Liveryman but one which is given to an outstanding working craftsman. He is currently enhancing his stone carving skills by undertaking a one year part-time course in Historic Stone Carving at The City & Guilds Art School in London.

Alan is one of a team of ten stonemasons working on a major repair programme at Salisbury Cathedral which primarily involves replacing the decayed stone fabric. This restoration began in 1985 and is scheduled to be completed by 2015; such major renovations are carried out approximately every 100 years. The cathedral was built over 750 years ago from locally quarried Chilmark limestone. An equivalent stone from Chicksgrove is being used for the restoration, as the Chilmark quarry is now closed.

At the outset, the architect produces a photogrammetric drawing of each elevation, and after consultation with the head mason, marks and numbers the most decayed stone that is required to be replaced or conserved. The mason's work is divided broadly into three parts: setting out, banker work, and fixing. At Salisbury they spend four months on each. Setting out is critical and involves accurately measuring and taking profiles of each old stone and drawing appropriate templates using geometry. This may involve cutting away the mortar around each stone and inserting a thin transparent orange plastic sheet, on which is marked the profile of the stone. If the stone is too decayed, it is necessary to take the profile by reference to adjacent stones. The templates, along with other measurements, enable full-scale drawings to be made of the three-dimensional piece. Banker work entails the precise cutting and shaping of the new stone, following the information on the templates. This takes place in the banker shop - named after the carpet-covered work bench on which the stone is worked. Any decorative stone ornament which requires replacement is also carved by the mason. Fixing involves the removal of the decayed stone and its replacement with the newly-worked piece. An architect-specified lime mortar mix is used to bed the stone. Most of the old stone is removed to a depth of 5-6 inches from the ashlar wall line, or whatever is deemed structurally permissible.

Jim Turley - Brick Maker

Jim is a senior brick maker at Coleford Brick and Tile and has worked for them for more than 30 years, having learned the craft with the company.

Established in 1925, this family owned business is located in the Forest of Dean in Worcestershire. Huw Gilson, the Managing Director, explained how the locally sourced clay is dug from seams near the surface, each layer having a slightly different quality. It is then transported to the yard, stacked seam upon seam, thereby forming a large mound. To make a batch of bricks, a cross-section of the mound is cut and processed in a pan-mill where water is added and mixed with the clay. In this way a uniform quality is maintained. The clay is then extruded and cut into clods, each clod having the correct amount of clay for one brick, and transported to the throwing table.

Making a brick first requires a mould of the correct shape to be constructed with due allowance being made for the 18% shrinkage that will occur after the brick has been dried and fired. These moulds are traditionally made from wood, so will eventually wear out and need to be replaced. Jim, who is known as a thrower, takes a clod, pats it into shape, and covers it with sand which will eventually give the brick its desired texture and colour. The clod is then thrown, literally, into the mould with sufficient force for it to spread out to take up the correct shape so as to leave no voids. The mould is then inverted, the brick released and stacked on a board. The stack of bricks is then placed onto the drying frame where it is partially air dried and then placed in a humidity dryer at 170°C for 36 hours. After this, they are hand-stacked into the kiln and fired for 70 hrs up to a maximum of 1,000°C, then allowed to cool. Before entry into the kiln the bricks are still 'green' (the original clay colour). After firing, the sand vitrifies and gives the brick its final colour.

The moulds are fabricated on site and both stock and special sizes are made. In the industry there are several standard brick sizes but Coleford will make any size and shape a customer specifies. Although they sell mainly to wholesalers, many high profile architects use their bricks, both for new projects and the renovation of historic buildings. Coleford recently supplied over 160,000 bricks and 14,000 specials for the reconstruction and remodelling of the Royal Shakespeare Theatre in Stratford on Avon.

The lead time from ordering is generally 4-6 weeks. A skilled brick maker can produce up to 1,500 hand thrown bricks per day and Coleford can produce up to 30,000 bricks in a week. There are two kilns holding 12,000 and 14,000 bricks respectively. Whilst this cannot compare with machine made bricks where a production rate of 40,000 per day is common, the machine made product cannot compare with a handmade brick, which has a unique aesthetic quality.

Mike Abbott - Greenwood Worker

Mike studied Combined Science at university, but having enjoyed working with wood from early childhood, it soon became clear to him that this was where his future lay. On leaving university he had a variety of municipal jobs which included a course on Recreational Management during which he investigated the advantages of using woodland for recreation. After a period working in Germany he returned to the UK and became a Youth Training Supervisor in Abbots Leigh, the village in which he grew up. His brief was to keep teenagers off the street and he began by teaching them what he himself was passionate about - working with green wood, particularly using a pole-lathe.

In 1985 he set up a business in Bristol called Living Wood Training and, after several moves, settled at his present location at Brookhouse Wood in Herefordshire. From May to September Mike runs woodland courses which attract participants from all over the world. I visited him in early summer. The venue was beautiful - approached via a country lane, through an isolated farm, along a track, across several fields and into a wood before emerging into a clearing. Here Mike has his open-air covered workshop, surrounded by accommodation huts - all built out of wood, of course. Facilities are available for up to seven students who attend a four-day course and make their own ladder-back chair and in the process learn to make and use a pole lathe.

Mike has refined and developed the local tradition of making these chairs. The frame comprises the back and front legs, seat rails, spindles and back slats. Students start with good quality unseasoned logs, cut from the surrounding woods. These logs are split (cleaved) along their natural grain to give maximum strength before being shaped using a variety of hand-tools and by turning on a pole-lathe. Other components are bent as required using a steam heater. The chair is then assembled using very tight joints formed naturally from the uneven shrinkage of the greenwood.

No machinery is used other than that which can be set up in a remote woodland workshop, which includes the use of a pole-lathe. Unlike a conventional lathe in which the wood is continuously turned in one direction by an electric motor, a pole-lathe is powered by the energy stored in a long pole when it is bent (see centre photograph). The pole is fixed at one end and supported somewhere along its length. A piece of cord is tied to the end of the pole, passed around the piece of wood to be turned, and tied onto the end of the foot treadle. As the treadle is pressed down, the wood turns in one direction, and when released it rotates in the opposite direction. This simple tool can be set up anywhere and has been the basis of woodland craft for centuries.

Mike is the author of *Green Woodwork* published in 1989 and more recently *Living Wood - From buying a woodland to making a chair* first published in 2002.

Jeremy Atkinson - Clog Maker

Jeremy was taught to make traditional clogs by, as he says, "a man who was taught by a man who was taught by a man". He has since passed on his skills to Geraint Parfitt, a demonstrating craftsman at the National Museum of Wales, although Jeremy remains the only traditional hand-carver in England. His workshop is in a small town in Herefordshire but he reaches the world through the internet. His clogs are individually made to measure and are worn by people who want hard-wearing comfortable footwear and those who might need more sole support than is afforded by more conventional boots. Clogs are excellent footwear for use in all weathers and have very low environmental impact. This is important to Jeremy, having been close to the self-sufficiency movement in the 1970's and, in more recent times, aware of the move to conserve natural resources.

English clogs have always been made from wood and leather. The key to achieving a well balanced clog lies largely in the wooden sole, and the quality of the leather uppers. Jeremy hand carves the wooden soles - he feels machine cutting compromises the three dimensional shape - using centuries-old traditional tools such as Stock Knife, Hollower, Twca Cam (little knife) and Gripper Bit.

The main picture shows the stock knife being used. He uses cherry and sycamore cut green out of a cleaved (split) trunk of between 6 and 8 inches in diameter. Cleaving allows the wood to be split along the grain. Shrinkage is minimal in sycamore and in bygone days sycamore clogs could be cut from the tree and finished the same day. Jeremy hand-cuts and dyes the leather himself, usually cow hide, but the traditional black waxed kip was from Indian water buffalo. Both leathers are between 2 and 4 mm thick and waterproof. Jeremy's clogs are expected to last for 6 to 12 years.

The peak of English clog making occurred during the Victorian era when they were the traditional footwear for factory workers - the original industrial boot. In heavy industry, particularly where the floor was likely to be strewn with hot metal, clogs were the only form of safe and reliable footwear.

Martin Buckle - Bee Skep Maker

A former biology teacher, Martin has kept bees for most of his adult life, having had up to 50 hives at any one time. As part of his biology lessons he installed several hives for the children to study and to learn about bees. Now retired, he judges at numerous shows including the National Honey Show and the Royal Highland Show in Edinburgh. He claims to be one of the very few active skep makers in England. He demonstrates his skills at craft fairs, agricultural shows and basket making events. He also runs bee skep making courses.

Martin has long been interested in the history of beekeeping and was introduced to bee skep making by chance when he was part of a group assisting with the making of a 17th century farm used in a TV series. As he was the only experienced beekeeper in the community he decided to make some bee skeps to fit into a garden wall. He was fascinated by this ancient form of beehive although he had never made one before. Bee skeps were used until about 150 years ago before the invention of the modular hive which allowed honeycombs to be removed without causing damage. Nonetheless the traditional bee skep is still used in some parts of Holland and Germany where beekeepers sell heather honey in the honeycomb. Keeping bees in skeps tends to encourage swarming, a practice favoured in times past as it increased the chances of beekeepers adding to their stock. Nowadays however, the efficiency of honey production is the most important factor. Nonetheless, the traditional bee skep has its place as it is acknowledged to be the best way of capturing a swarm. Bees seem to know instinctively that the skep is the correct size to accommodate their swarm and its rough interior surface makes it easier for them to cling onto. If the same size cardboard box was used it is likely the bees would enter to inspect, but be less likely to stay. If it rains, a skep is definitely preferred - imagine handling a wet soft cardboard box that is full of bees.

To make a skep, Martin first collects straw, grass, reeds or similar materials and makes a bundle about an inch in diameter. He starts by bending the end to form a flat ring, binding the bundle with bramble, cane or willow strips into a spiral. Adding more straw as needed, he creates a container about 12 to 14 inches in diameter and about 18 inches high, the shape being formed as work progresses. The bramble strips are made by stripping the thorns, splitting the wood in half, then in half again and finally removing the pith. The main hand-tool used is a Fid, a form of hollow needle traditionally made from bone. The fid is inserted through the straw such that each bramble stitch is pushed under a stitch in the previous circuit, thus binding the wreath of straw together and forming a very strong interlocked structure.

Seumas Campbell - Dry Stone Dyker

Seumas works on the Isle of Skye and became a dyker (the Scottish term for a drystone waller) by accident. His family have been crofters for several generations. When he was a teenager, his father suggested he went on a dyke-building course which was being run on the other side of the island so that he could repair one of their dykes which had fallen down. 20 years later Seumas is dyking professionally and is one of only 13 dykers in Scotland who are qualified as a Master Craftsman of The Dry Stone Walling Association. He is also an Examiner for the Association.

Dry stone walling in Britain began more than 3000 years ago and is generally considered to have originated in the Orkney Islands and in the Iron Age brochs (hollow-walled roundhouses) of North West Scotland where there was an abundance of surface rocks covered by a very thin layer of soil. The early walls had one stone side with earth packed over the other side. This was the style used in the Isle of Skye until the 17th century when The Clearances began, in which landowners forcibly removed the crofters in order to graze their sheep. They brought in shepherds from the mainland who built the walls and it is they who introduced the present design of two stone sides with smaller stones as rubble in between.

Dry stone walls rely on the skill of the builder rather than cement to keep them together. When making a wall, the topsoil is first removed and the largest, ugliest, stones are used as the foundation. These are laid with their longest sides across the width of the wall and the space between filled with small rocks, known as harting, in such a way as to ensure the large stones are held down firmly. The wall is then built up as described earlier; the skill lying in the selection of the best stone to sit on the one below. If long stones are available these are placed across the width of the wall at intervals to give added strength. The base is normally two and a half feet wide, and the sides are tapered such that the width at the top, just below the coping stones is half that of the base. A-frames are made and erected at each end of the wall and a line tied between them at the working height to act as a guide.

Seumas almost always uses recycled stone as, although there are working quarries in the area, newly-blasted stone is not suitable. The pictures show a new wall being built for a private house in Flodigarry, Northern Skye, the stone (basalt) coming from a recently demolished building in the same village. Whilst the initial cost of a dyke is greater than that of a fence, a wall is a sustainable product using natural materials and will last more than a lifetime whilst at the same time offering shelter and creating a habitat for plants, birds and animals.

Seumas constructed the camera obscura at Lochmaddy in North Uist, shown on page 44

Top: Murdo Lamont assisting Seumas Campbell

Darrell Hill - Willow Coffin Maker

Darrell is a third generation member of the Hill family who run The Somerset Willow Company in Bridgewater. He joined the family business as a teenager and has recently been appointed a Yeoman of the Worshipful Company of Basketmakers. His son has now joined the company and is undergoing the five year apprenticeship required of all their craftsmen.

For 50 years they have made traditional and contemporary willow baskets, always seeking to meet any demand for new products. In the 1950's they started to make picnic and pigeon baskets but just as the pigeon basket market started to decline they were fortunate to be asked to make a hot air balloon basket for Cameron Balloons of Bristol. Willow proved to be the perfect material as it is extremely strong, shock absorbent and does not deform during touch-down. The company now makes hot air balloon baskets for clients world-wide. When I visited their premises they were making a 4.5m long basket destined for a tourist company in South Africa. Their largest basket however was a double-decker unit made to hold 50 people.

Currently their most popular product is the willow coffin, perhaps the ultimate in environmental recycling and preservation of resources. The company had made their first coffin in 1998 and, in 2000, Darrell made one for his mother who died of cancer. Three years later when Adam Faith died the company were asked to supply a willow coffin. From that time this part of the business dramatically increased.

Each coffin has a woven base with wooden battens. The sides are then woven in the same way as a traditional basket. Each coffin is custom made, both for size and decoration. As with all basket work, the willow is soaked before use and then kept covered during the weaving process to ensure it does not dry out.

Willow is a renewable crop which can be harvested annually from the same crown which may last up to 60 years. The company owns their own willow farm on the Somerset Levels where this crop has been grown for centuries. It is cut at different stages, depending on the length required. The natural colour of the willow is determined by the colour of the bark and is generally light orange. White willow is produced by immersing the freshly cut saplings in water where they remain dormant; the following year they start to bud and at this point the bark is stripped and the willow boiled. For decorative purposes some of it is dyed using water-based dyes.

Robert Hurford - Wheelwright

From a very early age Robert has always wanted to make wheels, much encouraged by his engineer father. In 1968 he embarked on a course in Rural Studies, chosen as it was the only one he could find which incorporated some element of craft. He then taught for a few years before becoming a full-time wheelwright and is now a Liveryman of the Worshipful Company of Wheelwrights. His main business is the restoration of wheels for old vehicles such as ceremonial coaches and vintage cars, the former having wheels which may be hundreds of years old. For over 20 years he has also made carriages and similar vehicles for the film and TV industry. In 2001 he had a chance phone call from Channel 4 asking him to make five chariots, followed later in the day by the BBC wanting a reconstruction of a chariot as part of a programme on the excavation of a 2500 year old iron-age chariot at Wetwang in Yorkshire. Indeed Robert generally describes himself as a Chariot Maker. The film business has declined recently, but there is a continued demand for wheels for carriages, hearses, vintage cars and occasionally old farm vehicles. In 1997 Robert published a book in collaboration with John Wright entitled *Making a Wheel - How to make a Traditional Light English Pattern Wheel.*

The origins of the wheel are obscure. Stone Age man knew that a rolling stone or a round piece of wood moved an object more easily than one which had to be pulled or pushed. The first wheels were solid discs, carved out of one piece of wood although these had two disadvantages - they were heavy and they broke across the grain of the wood. The answer to the problem of how to reduce weight and yet retain strength came with the spoked wheel, known to have been in existence in Asia Minor by 2000 BC. The rims of these early wheels were made from one or two pieces of wood, bent to a full circle.

Wheelwrights were craftsmen of a high order, apparently using neither mathematical formulae nor even drawings. Their knowledge and experience of the craft was passed from father to son, from master to apprentice.

The modern wooden wheel has a hub - or stock - which is generally made from elm; the spindles, or spokes from oak and the rim from ash. The rim is made from a number of segments, each known as a felloe and bound with steel. Tenons are made at each end of the spoke to insert into the hub and into the felloe. In Robert's workshop there were numerous chariot wheels in various states of completion or repair and he demonstrated how each piece fitted together with great precision. A well made wheel should last for 150 years given proper care and maintenance.

Charles Hutcheon - Stick Maker

Twenty years ago Charles visited the Hebridean island of Islay and, on a whim, purchased a kit, (a piece of antler and wooden stick) and so made his first stick. A few years later he discovered the British Stickmakers Guild at a country fair and entered a competition where he gained first and third prizes. This unexpected result prompted him to join the Guild, of which he is now Secretary. There are approximately 2000 UK members plus some fifty from overseas. Some members make sticks as a hobby, others collect them and many attend fairs where their products are sold. To derive a living from the craft is difficult if not impossible.

Fundamentally the stick is a walking aid; references to their use date from biblical times. Nowadays, they are widely used by hikers as well as by the elderly needing a little additional support. Hiking sticks are longer and known as hiking staffs or thumb-sticks. Designs are very wide-ranging, many having intricately carved handles made from a variety of materials. Charles's thumb-sticks frequently incorporate a compass or a whistle in the antler handle. The shank, or shaft is typically made from hazel which is easily obtained and grows reasonably straight. However, sweet chestnut, holly, blackthorn and fruitwood are also used. The wood is always cut in December or January and seasoned before use. The shaft usually requires to be straightened to some extent, particularly for competitions, a process achieved by using steam.

Charles generally uses antler horn from Islay for his handles but has also used horn from rams, cows and buffalo as well as various types of wood. The Islay antlers are predominantly from red deer, but may also come from roe and fallow deer. They shed their antlers each year and every year the new horns grow larger, thus horns from older deer have more branches. These will, of course, make more handles. Deer antler is bone and cannot be shaped or bent, so the shape of the handle relies on careful selection. Ramshorn and buffalo horn on the other hand are cartilage. In their natural state these horns are highly curved but, by careful application of heat and very high pressures, they can be bent into the required shape before being cut. Buffalo horn is solid, whereas ramshorn is hollow and again, using heat and high pressure, it can be compressed until it is solid. Only then can it be worked into the required shape. One can but marvel at the skill of the stick makers of ancient times who fashioned the classical shepherd's crook.

Owen Jones
Oak Swill Basket Maker

In 1988 Owen was introduced to a retired 'Swiller' called John Barker who used to work in a swill shop in Broughton-in-Furness, Cumbria. John was one of the last of his generation of oak swill basket makers and taught Owen the craft; now Owen is the only person left making them. He is concerned that the craft should continue and is currently training two young women. Oak swill baskets are traditional to the southern Lake District and have been made in the same area for centuries. This type of basket takes on different names when sold elsewhere in Northern Britain. For example, they are known as Skeps in Yorkshire, Wiskets in Cheshire, Skips in the North East and Tatty baskets or Sculls in Scotland. Their origins are unclear but they are thought to have evolved as a cottage industry which then became a trade in its own right after the Industrial Revolution.

A century ago they were used to carry coal to the boilers on steam ships. Owen originally sold to traditional customers such as farmers who had used these baskets for generations for a variety of tasks such as broadcasting seed and transporting potatoes and animal feed. This market ceased and nowadays they are more likely to be found carrying garden produce, logs, laundry or used as cradles. Owen travels to shows around the country giving demonstrations and selling his baskets. He also runs three-day courses in which students start with an oak log and a hazel rod and end up with a finished swill.

When Owen first started in business he obtained his oak and hazel from a local man called Bill Hogarth, the last true coppice merchant in the area. When Bill died, Owen had to source the timber himself and now coppices the wood in the nearby Rusland valley. As a result he also sells firewood, makes besom brooms and charcoal to sell locally.

To make the swills he fells oak and uses the first ten feet of the trunk which he cuts into logs varying in length from 2-5ft. The smaller diameter logs are cleft into quarters along their length, the larger ones into eighths. These pieces are known as billets. They are boiled in water for several hours and, whilst still hot, are taken one by one and riven along the grain using a riving knife. The shorter lengths, called spelks, form the ribs of the baskets and are shaped, or dressed using a draw knife, whilst being held in the jaws of a mare (a foot-operated clamp). The longer lengths, called taws, are split and shaved whilst being held on the knee using a hand knife. The rim or 'bool' of the basket is made from hazel which has been steamed for twenty minutes before being bent into the characteristic shape. The ribs are then attached to it and the taws woven in whilst still damp. It takes several hours to make one basket.

Peter Jones - Charcoal Maker

Twenty years ago, Peter left his job as a foreman with an agricultural contractor. A chance discussion on the quality of charcoal used for barbecues prompted him to think that he could make charcoal for a living. He spent two weeks with a local charcoal maker, after which he built his own kiln; however, it took a further two years to fully master the techniques and reliably produce charcoal for sale. In those early days he had a business partner and two assistants operating eight kilns; however, with the growing popularity of gas-fired barbecues, he now operates one kiln on his own. Peter thinks that there are perhaps 200 charcoal makers in the country, although he is now one of the last in East Kent and certainly one of the few providing hog roasts using his own charcoal as fuel. His business also supplies logs and kindling to local customers. For the last ten years he has rented an area of woodland from the Ministry of Defence; his age-old craft being carried out within a mile of the entrance to the Channel Tunnel.

Peter's charcoal is made in the traditional way using a sustainable supply of coppiced wood which he cuts himself. This is a method of woodland management whereby the tree is cut to the ground from whence new shoots grow. Peter uses ash cut into lengths of approximately six feet and having a diameter of between three to nine inches. The kiln is made of steel, four feet high and eight feet across; has no base (it rests on the ground) and has a domed metal cover. There are four air intakes around the base and four outlets into which chimneys are inserted. The number and size of air intakes controls the rate of burning which is essential for the production of top quality charcoal.

Before filling the kiln with green wood, a pole about six inches diameter - known as a pin - is placed upright in the centre and secured; this will later be removed. Charred wood is put around the pin before green logs are cut and split and put randomly in the kiln. Some charcoal makers prefer to stack the wood in an orderly fashion, and, whilst that may allow a greater number of logs to be used, Peter believes his method is more efficient. Filling takes about two hours after which the pin is removed and burning newspaper dropped into the hole where the charred wood was placed. The four chimneys are placed in position and the wood starts to burn; when this has fully ignited the kiln cover is placed on top. When the cover drops it is then sealed around the edges using sand. The kiln is left for 24 hours during which time all volatile material is removed from the wood as indicated by the emission turning to a light blue colour. At this point both the chimneys and the air intakes are fully sealed and the kiln allowed to cool for a further day. The charcoal is then removed, graded and bagged.

The kiln holds three tonnes of logs and produces about three hundred kilogrammes of charcoal. Peter produces about 6 tonnes of charcoal per year.

Terry Kenny - Coracle Maker

From an early age, Terry messed about in small boats, so it was not surprising that, when he moved to Shropshire some twenty years ago he attended a course on coracle making, run by the Greenwood Centre (part of the Small Woods Association) in Coalbrookdale near Ironbridge. Following this course, Terry began to assist the tutors, later becoming a course tutor himself, such is his enthusiasm for this ancient form of river craft. He is chairman of the Coracle Society, an organisation whose primary aim is to promote the study, construction and collection of coracles, curraghs and similar craft.

A coracle is a small lightweight river boat, whose generic oval shape is often likened to half a walnut shell. Each coracle is unique in design and tailored to the river conditions in the region where it is built. Some are more square and stable, whereas others are more bowl-shaped and manoeuvrable. Their common feature is their very shallow draught, being able to be used in only a few inches of water. Indeed, one of their original uses in the Welsh Marches near Ironbridge was for the capture of rabbits from flooded fields; rabbits would migrate to the higher parts of the land only to be caught by locals using their coracles in the surrounding shallow water. Although traditionally used in Wales, coracles are also found in the west of England and in Scotland.

Originally, coracles were made from willow or hazel rods covered with skins. Whilst this method is still used occasionally, modern coracles more commonly use heavy duty calico stretched over a frame of sawn ash and waterproofed with bitumastic paint. The ash strips are interwoven to form the basic structure, the overall shape of which is determined by the shape of the outer rim. The wooden seat is secured slightly off centre to ensure the correct balance. Some modern coracles are made from fibreglass.

Most of those attending Terry's courses make coracles purely for leisure activities -indeed, the recent increase in their interest stems from this use. They are light and thus easily carried by one person, and easy to store. They can be manoeuvred with one hand and of course can be sailed on the shallowest of water.

Adam King - Besom Broom Maker

It is not surprising that Adam has made woodworking his career, as his grandfather was a furniture maker in High Wycombe and his father used to demonstrate wood turning using a pole lathe at craft fairs, often accompanied by the seven year old Adam. He learnt to make besom brooms whilst attending these fairs and was soon giving demonstrations. He believes there are now very few others in the country practising this ancient craft.

There are two components to the broom; the head and the handle. The head is made from birchwood, coppiced after 3-4 years and cut in the winter when the sap is down. This is bundled together and stored for about a year to season. It is harvested locally from heathland on nearby Stoke Poges Common as part of the land management programme. Birch trees require to be removed periodically as they are a primary coloniser - they will be amongst the first plants to grow on previously barren ground. The handles are made from hazel stripped of its bark whilst green and seasoned for a month - the wood also obtained locally. Adam collects enough wood in the winter to meet his needs throughout the year.

To make a broom the birchwood bundle is bound very tightly with wire (willow strips are sometimes used instead by request). The handle is then pointed and rammed into the centre of the birch bundle and secured with a hardwood wedge. The besom broom is still accepted as the best tool for general outdoor garden use and particularly for clearing worm casts from a new lawn without any danger of damaging the grass.

The other, very different, half of Adam's business is making Welsh Love Spoons - each one elaborately carved from a single piece of wood. According to Welsh folklore, these ornate spoons were traditionally made by young men as a love token for their sweethearts. The earliest surviving example dates from around 1667 and is on display at the Welsh Folk Museum in Cardiff.

The design of each spoon is created and drawn on paper which is then secured to a piece of wood – usually limewood, as it has a very even grain. Adam uses a horizontal fretsaw made by his father to cut out the elaborate pattern. The back of the spoon is then rounded using a miniature spokeshave. He then uses a selection of gouges, flat chisels, v-shaped chisels and carving knives to complete the carving. Adam has over a hundred of these tools although only about twenty are commonly used. After a careful final sanding, the spoon is ready for sale.

Adam sells at craft fares in the UK and also receives commissions and orders from many countries around the world; the internet enabling his craft to remain a viable business.

Richard Lewis - Hedge Layer

Richard's father, and both grandfathers were hedge layers and so it is not surprising that he is following the family tradition. However, it was a friend who suggested he accompany him to a hedge laying competition, and who later taught him the craft that started his career. Richard is now an accredited Master Craftsman of the National Hedge Laying Society. He enters up to ten competitions each year and became the Welsh champion in 1996 and 2010.

Hedge laying declined after WW2 due to lack of labour and the introduction of farming machinery. By the 1960's hedges were rapidly disappearing as farming economics dictated fewer, larger, fields. As a result, in 1978, the National Hedge Laying Society was formed to ensure that the ancient skills of hedge management were not lost forever. In 1997, legislation was introduced to protect the hedgerows and encourage farmers and landowners to manage existing hedges for conservation as a wildlife habitat. Hedge maintenance is now part of good farming practice and the skills of the hedge layer are in great demand. The season starts in October when the leaves begin to fall and the sap is moving down; and extends until March.

Where farmers keep cattle or sheep in fields, a good well maintained hedge is essential; cattle tend to lean against a hedge and sheep will push through the base. Left unmanaged, a hedgerow will grow upwards and outwards, eventually becoming a line of trees. There are over a dozen distinct hedge laying styles used in different parts of the country, within which are many local variations depending upon the type of livestock and hedging plants used. However, regardless of the region, the basic elements remain the same.

Richard is based in Wales, but when I met him he was working on a hedge in Shropshire. Watching him work is to witness a transformation. First he assesses the overgrown hedge to decide which plant stems to cut out and which to leave. Using a chainsaw or a correctly sharpened axe, a cut is made approximately three-quarters of the way through each stem enabling it to be bent over to an angle of about 35°; these are then called pleachers. The depth of the cut is critical - it must be sufficient to allow the pleacher to be positioned, but not so deep as to cut into the bast or cambium layers. In this way the pleacher is still attached by a thin piece of wood and can therefore continue to grow. Stakes or posts are driven into the ground at intervals of between 18-24 inches to act as supports. These are usually positioned at an angle of 55-80° depending on the style being used and the pleachers woven between them. In Welsh styles, deadwood pleachers are also incorporated at intervals, covering the stumps to stop sheep eating the new growth. Smaller shoots branching off the pleachers, known as 'brush', are either woven between them or cut off using a bill hook. Finally, hazel heatherings are woven along the top of the hedge between the stakes; any protruding stakes being sawn off, leaving the finished hedge about 3½ feet high. A laid hedge would be expected to last for 15-20 years or more with only minimum maintenance.

Shaun Linsley
Cane Fishing Rod Maker

Shaun started fishing when he was 13 years old. Limited funds meant that he could only afford to buy cane rods, whose price had dropped with the advent of the more popular ones made from fibreglass. He used the cane rods, repairing them when necessary, and found there was a ready market for his repaired or renovated rods. So successful was this venture that he decided to make his own rods and, in 1993, set up his business. He also teaches children who have been excluded from school, and as a fishing enthusiast, brings this knowledge to his teaching. He deals with fairly unruly children, teaching them how to make a rod and taking them fishing. For many this is their first experience of 'normal life' and he finds they become totally absorbed. He shows them that there is an alternative to always being in trouble.

Despite carbon fibre now being the material of choice for most fishermen, there is still a strong demand for cane rods. By the very nature of the material, cane (bamboo) allows better transmission of vibrations from the line, an important element for the discerning fisherman when playing the fish. A quality cane rod requires the best possible cane. There are many sources of this material, although the best comes from Tonkin in China. Shaun buys his cane in 13ft lengths and seasons them for 15 years, replenishing his stock every five years.

To make a rod, the (approximately) one and a half inch diameter cane is split in half, and each half then further split into three. Each length of split cane is heated to remove moisture and to facilitate straightening; removing moisture is essential otherwise the rod will not return to its original shape after bending. The natural surface enamel is removed and the wood planed to produce a length which is an equilateral triangle in section. Since a rod tapers uniformly from about one and a half inches at the reel end to about one quarter of an inch at the far end, each length has to be planed to achieve the taper whilst still retaining the triangular section. Shaun has developed a vice whose jaws are shaped to the appropriate angle (60 degrees) and which is adjustable along its length to allow the taper to be achieved. All work is carried out using hand tools only.

When the six segments have been prepared they are glued together to form the rod which is hexagonal in section. After attaching the various fittings, the rod is varnished; each coat applied as the rod slowly rotates, thereby giving a uniform finish.

Each hand-made Shaun Linsley rod is produced to the customer's specifications, many of whom purchase a pair of rods - in which case they are both made from the same piece of cane. Although some consider them collector's items, Shaun likes to think they will be used for sport.

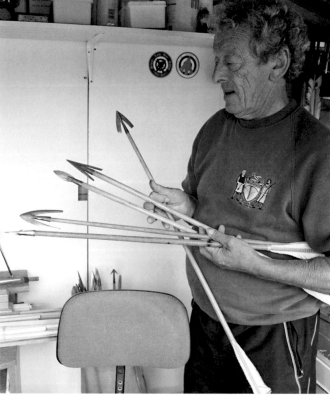

Mike Manns - Fletcher

Some years ago Mike accompanied his daughter to the Bosworth Show as she wanted to take archery lessons. At that time, he was looking for a new occupation, and a friend, John Randall, a Master Bowyer and Fletcher, suggested he might be interested in making arrows and offered to take him on as an apprentice Fletcher. Some years later, Mike was invited to become a member of the Worshipful Company of Bowyers, of which he is now a Freeman. He is also a member of the 'Bowmen of Bosworth' an association dedicated to the use of the longbow. They re-enact the Battle of Bosworth in Leicestershire, more commonly known as the War of the Roses. The battle took place on 22nd August 1485 and ended 30 years of English civil war in which the longbow was the main weapon and a large number of arrows were therefore required.

The apprenticeship teaches students to make traditional wooden arrows for any bow rather than the high tech arrows used in competitive tournaments such as the Olympics where carbon fibre is the material of choice. At the end of the two and a half years study, Mike was required to produce a box fitted out to take twelve different arrows, each demonstrating a specific aspect of the craft. A standard arrow is 31½ inches long although archers will specify different lengths according to their arm and bow length. The length required is determined by the distance from the out-stretched finger tip to the chest. An arrow naturally bends in flight as a result of the force applied to its end as the energy of the bow pushes the arrow forward. The amount of bend (the spine) is calculable and the arrow diameter has to be correct to ensure the spine can be achieved. Poplar is often used as it is a light yet strong wood.

In days of old arrow heads would have been made for specific purposes ranging from piercing armour in battle, causing horses to fall by deflecting from their legs, or for hunting. Although used for different reasons, modern arrow heads are similarly diverse. The heads may be cast out of iron, fashioned out of brass, or merely sharpened to a point; rubber heads are usually used for re-enactment shows. The arrows have three feathers at the end to stabilise the flight path. These must all be of the same quality and type, those from goose or swan considered the best. The three feathers are positioned equidistantly around the shaft.

Although some groups of archers hunt, most arrows are made for shooting at targets. A significant number are made for presentation or ceremonial purposes, where they may be highly decorative. Serious archers have arrows made to their specific requirements; they are often marked with a colour code which is unique to the owner.

Rod Miller - Thatcher

After leaving school, Rod served an apprenticeship in thatching, and on completion became the resident thatcher on the Weld Estate in Lulworth. At that time (1966), there were approximately 600 thatchers in the country, over half of whom were over retirement age. Rod was concerned that the craft should survive, so in 1967 he became one of the founder members of the National Society of Master Thatchers, of which he is currently chairman. He started his own business in 1966 and now has a workforce of 8 people. He is well known in thatching circles as a committed campaigner for the industry and was instrumental in getting the industry associated with the Partners in Technology Project (funded by the industry and the then Department of the Environment, Transport and the Regions)

In principle, any grass or long-stemmed plant can be used to thatch a roof. In the distant past when there were extensive wetlands, water reed was commonly used and is still the preferred material. Straw was also used, being a by-product of cereal crops. However, modifications to seed stocks, made in order to increase wheat yield, has reduced the stem length rendering it largely unsuitable for thatching. In earlier years, Rod grew his own wheat straw and purchased locally-grown water reed. However, sourcing sufficient quantities became difficult, particularly in the 1980's when the local reed beds were sold to be maintained as a nature reserve. At the same time, the number of reed beds in Norfolk also decreased, as did the quality of reed being produced; it thus became necessary to seek alternative sources. Nowadays he imports reed and during my visit his barn held considerable stocks, purchased from Turkey.

Rod prefers to use water reed because, in his experience, this will give his customers a roof that will last longer than one thatched using either wheat straw or long straw. In the UK, most reed is cut by machine, but it is still possible to obtain hand-cut reed from Turkey. With a roof pitch of 45 degrees, a reed thatch would be expected to last 30 to 40 years, although some have lasted much longer. Typically, straw thatch has a life expectation of 15 to 20 years, or longer in some parts of the country.

Rod uses some 300,000 bundles of water reed each year, each bundle having a circumference of approximately 66cm and a length of one to two metres. When thatching, the bundle is opened out and pinned to the roof, one bundle covering approximately 0.1 square metres. It is fixed using either hazel rods or steel bars, with either steel crooks driven into the rafters or stainless steel wired screws fixed to the battens or rafters. The wired screws do very little damage to either the timber, or the fireboard, which is used more these days. Spar coating is the method of fixing either straw or reed to an existing layer of thatch. Spars made from coppiced hazel are split with a hook or an adze, then pointed at each end and twisted to form a U-shape. These are usually between 66cm and 76cm long. They are also used to form the decorative pattern on the ridge. Born and bred in the countryside, Rod has always had an interest in coppice work and also makes hurdle fences.

John Randall and Alan Rogers - Bowyers

John and Alan are Master Bowyers who work together under the name of Ambion Longbows. The name Ambion was taken from nearby Ambion Hill, on which the Battle of Bosworth was fought in 1485. John holds the gold certificate of the Worshipful Company of Bowyers which is awarded for services to bow making. This has been awarded on only three occasions. He started making bows many years ago when he was a member of Nottingham Archers and became regional champion using a steel bow. Alan is a Freeman of the same Company and holds their silver certificate which is awarded for excellence in bow making. They are both founder members of the Guild of Traditional Bowyers and Fletchers which they started in 1982 to ensure that the ancient craft of longbow making could continue. To become a member requires an apprenticeship of three years under a Master Bowyer and an examination of the work produced. After moving to Market Bosworth in 1975 John joined the Bowmen of Bosworth archery club where he met Alan. A club meeting was interrupted to watch the raising of the Mary Rose on television and, while looking at some of the discovered bows, they decided to create their own wooden ones. Several weeks later their first longbow was produced.

The arrow travelled a distance of 100 yards. After the second one was made they encountered problems which caused the next 10 or so to fail. This was mainly attributed to the choice of timber and there was a big learning curve relating to timber selection. Following discussion and experimentation a dramatic improvement resulted in all their bows being capable of propelling arrows a distance of 200 yards.

The length of a longbow is between 5 ft 6 in and 6 ft depending upon the height of the archer and length of arm. It is made entirely of wood, with yew being considered the most effective. Other woods are used, such as lemonwood, maple, laburnum and ash. The British Longbow Society now also accepts bamboo.

The bow section is D shaped with the flat side (the back) on the outside and the curved side (the belly) on the inside. The depth of the wood must never exceed 80% of the width otherwise expansion forces will exceed compression forces and the bow can be completely deformed. The back of the bow is made from sapwood and the belly from heartwood. Heartwood and sapwood have different physical properties. Heartwood performs better under compression; sapwood is better under tension. All these characteristics were noted in the bows recovered from the Mary Rose. Modern bows are sometimes laminated to achieve these properties. All bows have strengthened tips in which there is a groove called a 'nock' in which to place the string. These tips are made from bone or buffalo horn.

Alan and John prefer to use linen strings as these are traditional; however, man-made fibres are sometimes used. A string may contain between 12 and 16 separate threads depending upon the strength of the bow, the threads being bound together at the centre with cotton to create a smooth loose from the string for the fingers.

John and Graeme Rudd
Rake Makers

John Rudd's grandfather started the business in 1890 at a time when every village had its own blacksmith and carpenter. Wooden rakes were made on a seasonal basis, mainly for haymaking during June and July. Now, some 120 years later, John and his son Graeme are the only people left in this business and they continue to make rakes at the same premises in the village of Dufton in Cumbria. John learnt the craft from his father - as a child he would spend time in the workshop and learnt every aspect of the work. His son Graeme learnt carpentry at college after which he joined the family business. Some 90% of their annual production of 10,000 rakes goes to wholesalers in Coln and Wigan, the remainder being sold directly to customers in the north of England. The rakes are used primarily by people involved in public gardens and particularly for raking golf course bunkers and sports grounds.

A rake has four component parts - the shaft or handle, the head, the teeth and the bow. The shaft is made from ash imported from Germany. It needs to be knot free and straight grained. Although some ash can be obtained in England, it needs to be imported to achieve the quality required, as was the case in John's grandfather's time. The head - this holds the teeth - is made from English ash from Yorkshire. There are 16 teeth in each head, made from silver birch imported from Sweden. Finally the bow, the curved piece of wood used to secure the head to the handle, is also made from English ash. The bows are cut to length and boiled in water before being bent around a former. They are then placed on a rack to dry for two days before being ready for use.

The shaft is imported in square section and until the early 1970's was planed circular by hand; now a machine tool is used. John's father was always seeking to use the latest tools. In 1949 he had an engineer friend who designed and constructed a machine to drill the holes in the head, cut the teeth to length and then ram them into the head. This machine is still in constant use today. Finally, the teeth are pointed using a pointing machine, similar to an industrial pencil sharpener.

These rakes are made in batches of 80 dozen at a time, each batch taking several weeks to complete. The rake will last for at least 30 years and occasionally they are returned to be retoothed. Originally a buyer would order a number of spares, handles, teeth etc., but nowadays because they last so well no spares are supplied.

Alastair Simms - Cooper

Alastair began working as an apprentice Cooper on his sixteenth birthday and attained the rank of Master Cooper in 1994. He had always wanted to be a carpenter but after a short time working for a cooper it became clear that he had the right skills for such exacting work and he decided to concentrate on this craft instead. At that time there were thousands of qualified barrel makers across England but the emergence of modern metal casks saw the numbers decline. He is now the only Master Cooper in the country and there are only four breweries in the country still employing coopers. Having spent 16 years at Theakston's Brewery, Alastair currently works for Wadworth's Brewery in Devizes, a family run business established in 1875. He runs the cooperage on a commercial basis and also performs contract work for other breweries, cider makers and vineyards.

An apprentice works for four years under a Master, the first two spent using only hand-tools. After three years a there is a trade test following which the title of Journeyman Cooper is bestowed. To become a Master Cooper of the Worshipful Company of Coopers requires that the Journeyman trains an apprentice, thus the high standards of the craft are passed on to future generations. In Scotland however the rank of Master Cooper is given to anyone who owns their own distillery and cooperage.

Barrels are made from oak, and, although English oak was traditionally used, economics dictate that the wood is now imported. Oak barrels can have a working life of over 80 years, compared with stainless steel which typically lasts for around 30 years, (less if it becomes damaged). Ale barrels are made in different sizes, the largest and original as defined in 1454 being called a tun (which holds 252 gallons), followed more recently (in 1803) by a butt (108 gallons), a hogshead (54 gallons), a barrel (36 gallons), a kilderkin (18 gallons), a firkin (9 gallons) and a pin, holding 4.5 gallons. An oak barrel can be dismantled and the wood reused to make a smaller barrel, which in turn can be used to make an even smaller one. Thus the oak can have a working life in excess of 130 years.

Seasoned oak is split and the timber cut and carefully shaped into 20 pieces such that they fit together precisely. They are placed in a steam room to make the timbers more pliable for bending into shape. The heads are made from dowel-jointed oak planks and fitted onto the top and bottom of the barrel.

Not surprisingly, Alastair is an ale connoisseur, and has no doubt that beer stored in oak tastes best.

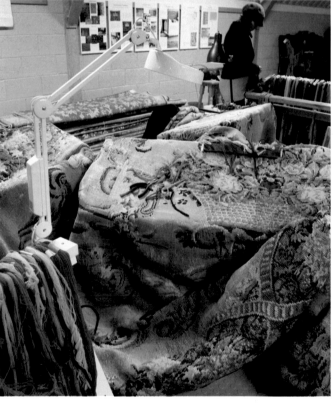

David Bamford
Carpet Designer & Colourist

After leaving school David joined a London photographic studio before deciding to travel the world. In Afghanistan he "discovered textiles" and decided that this was an area within which he would like to work. He now specialises in designing and producing carpets based on 18th century designs. He describes himself as 'A Master Weaver of Fine Quality Bespoke Handknotted Carpets and Flatweaves from Existing Historical Design & Colourings or Newly Drafted Designs & Colours to Suit'. In 1985/6 he was commissioned by the National Trust to investigate the possibility of reweaving large carpets as a positive conservation measure. The originals could then be put into storage, so that they were no longer walked upon by the public. The first of these was woven in Turkey, but a few years later an opportunity arose to take over a large workshop in Bulgaria where the carpets are now woven. From an original staff of 3-4 people with the necessary weaving skills he has built up his business and is now one of the only workshops weaving hand knotted classical carpets in Europe.

When commissioned to make a carpet for an important historic room, David will use his knowledge and experience to produce a design which is correct for the period. A black and white point drawing of sections of the carpet is then made to determine the pitch of the knots; for a good quality English carpet there will be approximately 100,000 knots per square metre. To establish the appropriate colour palette, David uses his archive of over 6000 sample tufts of wool, each of which have 5-6 colour variations, depending on the dye concentration. When the colours have been approved, a point drawing of the entire carpet is made, and then printed onto A4 sheets which are later used by the weavers.

Only the longest and very best 100% wool fibre with a diameter of 38-40 microns, specially sourced in the Rhodopi Mountains, is used, which gives the carpets the quality and longevity associated with hand woven English Axminster carpets of the 18th century. The spun wool is then carefully hand-dyed; the loom is strung with a cotton warp and woven with a wool weft. Each knot is made using the point paper drawing to determine the design. During the weaving process several people carefully rotate the roll to ensure the warp and weft remain exactly at right angles to each other - only in this way will the finished carpet lie perfectly flat.

Once the weaving is completed the carpet is cut off the loom and the pile hand-cut using scissors to give a uniform smooth finish. The finished pile length is between 10-12mm, compared with a conventional domestic carpet which has a 5-6mm pile length. Each row is painstakingly inspected and surplus wool removed with a comb; on an 8m wide carpet, this proceeds at the rate of approximately 1m per day. Such carpets can last for generations.

Jan Beaney - Textile Artist

Jan studied art after leaving school, graduating in Painting and Lithography. This was against the advice of her headmistress, but with the full support of her parents provided she did a year's teaching course to give her a secure job. In her final year at art school, she was introduced to the creative possibilities of stitch. She taught art at 'O' and 'A' level and very much enjoyed the experience. The school also allowed her to teach embroidery - unusual at the time when 'useful' skills were deemed more appropriate. Nonetheless, she enjoyed the challenge of learning the night before that which she would teach the next day, and, having gained her teaching qualifications, was 'hooked'. She has taught in various colleges and is now a freelance teacher in the UK and worldwide. Nothing changes - her enthusiasm remains infectious and she means what she says when she declares "I will never retire".

Jan concentrated on learning about British traditional embroidery as well as that from overseas; in 1963, she became a member of the 62 Group, an organisation set up to assist newly qualified artists to exhibit their work. The group, of which Jan is now an honorary member, has members from both home and abroad. Innovative exhibitions are held each year and these have been very influential in developing the awareness and respect for textile art.

In 1966, the Embroiderers' Guild was instrumental in finding a publisher who would commission her to write a book biased towards art rather than domestic embroidery. The result was her first book *The Young Embroiderer.* There followed numerous other publications, television series and videos. In 1983 she teamed up with one of her former students, Jean Littlejohn, to teach their art, each separately covering their own particular topic. Both art trained, they maintain quite different - but complementary - styles. In 1997 they set up Double Trouble Enterprises, publishing books to promote design and all aspects of stitched textiles. Their most recent book, *Stitchscapes* was published in 2010.

Jan's inspiration comes from what she sees around her, from the field "down the road" to landscapes on holiday or whilst teaching worldwide. She always starts by making an outline design in her sketchbook of that which has inspired her. She thinks about what element she wants to concentrate upon, understating or exaggerating certain aspects, before embarking on the work. Her aim is to create a simple image that captures the essence of the place. She frequently works with soluble film which is embroidered using applied fabric fragments, hand and or machine work. The base material is then removed by washing, to reveal a new cloth or a lace-like piece of textile art such as her 'Out of the Mist' (see picture), 102 x 78cm, mounted on canvas and inspired by a rape-seed field nearby. Jan only embroiders that which inspires her; she never works to commission although her art is sold through exhibitions and is in both private and public collections.

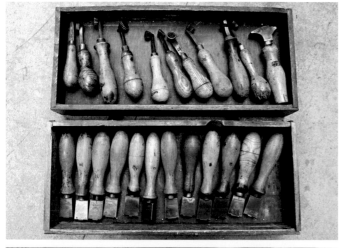

Deborah Carré & James Ducker
Shoemakers

Deborah has always had a passion for shoes; her mother had a fine collection and her father always insisted on polishing the family's footwear before church. She studied Fashion Design and Marketing at university after which she worked in marketing for a luxury goods manufacturer. However, wanting to be more hands-on, in 1997 she won a Queen Elizabeth Trust Scholarship which sponsored an apprenticeship with Paul Wilson, master shoemaker to the firm John Lobb Ltd of London. She then set up her own business, Atelier Carré, making bespoke shoes and bags. Deborah is a visiting lecturer in shoe and handbag design & marketing at the London College of Fashion, University of the Arts, London.

James had a family background in art and craft and lived in Spain, where he taught English. The father of one of his students was a prominent member of the shoe guild and taught shoemaking. In his spare time, James enrolled on two evening classes for making and for pattern cutting. On returning to London he too obtained an apprenticeship with John Lobb Ltd and also worked under the tutelage of Paul Wilson, where he met Deborah. On completing his training he continued as a freelance shoemaker and taught hand-sewn shoemaking at Cordwainers and The London College of Fashion. In 2004 Deborah and James went into partnership, forming carréducker to make bespoke shoes. They also run shoemaking courses in London and New York.

Making a hand-sewn shoe involves a number of specialised crafts. First, the colour and style is discussed with the client and careful measurements of each foot are taken. Using these measurements, a wooden last is made by a specialist in Northampton. This is then sent to Deborah and James, who draw the design of the shoe on it and send it to a pattern maker and closer. They break the design down into its component pieces and transfer the three-dimensional shape onto two-dimensional pieces of leather. In carrying out this task the hide is laid out in order to determine the best places from which to cut the patterns. The job of the closer is then to stitch all the pieces together to form the upper of the shoe. On completion of the upper, it is temporarily attached to the last and the client returns for the fitting; depending on the complexity of the feet, several such visits may be required. The last is adjusted accordingly, either adding or taking away material. Once a perfect fit is achieved, the shoes are made.

Deborah and James have the critical task of preparing the insole and attaching it to the upper (welting). The sole is then stitched to the welt using waxed thread hand twisted from hemp. Next the heel is built, lift by lift, and shaped with a knife. The final stage is to finish the heel, sole edges and sole, using rasps and sandpaper. No machines are used at any stage in making the shoe. Such is the reputation for English hand-made shoes that they have clients in USA, Australia and Europe as well as in the UK.

Anna Crutchley
Passementerie Maker

Anna studied textiles at West Surrey College of Art and Design and for ten years concentrated on hand-weaving fabrics, scarves and shawls. In 1983 she started to get commissions to weave braids and fringes and in 1989 a placement at the firm of G J Turner (Trimmings) Ltd., now Turner Trimmings, provided her with specialist training. In 1990 she again became self-employed working on both wide fabric weaving and trimmings. She has made trimmings for numerous organisations including Sir John Soane's Museum, the National Trust and for many interior designers, upholsterers and furniture restorers. She has written *The Tassels Book: An Inspirational Guide to Tassels and Tassel-making* and *Tassel Making: Revealing the Secrets of How to Make the World's Most Gorgeous Fabric Decorations*.

Anna's work currently involves cord spinning, weaving braids and fringes, and making tassels. She always works to commission creating pieces which are historically accurate. Cord spinning requires very long premises if long cords are required - known as ropewalks. Although she originally rented a ropewalk, when it ceased to be available she used her studio - plus the entire length of her house and garden. The strands of cord are anchored at one end, and attached to a rotating hand-tool at the other. The tension is maintained whilst the tool rotates and the cord is formed. Each strand of a cord may itself be a cord, having been similarly spun using many thin strands of thread. In this way a very wide range of colours, constructions and designs may be incorporated as required. Anna uses a narrow loom based on an 18th century model, to weave braids.

To make a basic tassel, yarn or high twist cords are wrapped around a wooden skirt-board a number of times depending on the fullness required. The board is removed and the bundle of yarn is tied tightly around a cord. The yarn is folded over and bound, and the loops at the bottom cut to form the skirt of the tassel. A more complex tassel involves the use of a specially shaped wooden head, covered with threads or wound with gimp, and maybe decorated with cords or beads. The skirts may be equally complex, dressed with smaller tassels, bullions (twisted loop skirts), with jasmin drops of beads covered in silk thread, or trellised cords.

Frances Kelly - Master Saddler

Frances has been a Master Saddler for about 30 years and has won many of the top prizes at the national Saddle and Bridle competitions, including Best in Show three times at the Society of Master Saddler's competition. She is a past president of the Society of Master Saddlers and now serves on its executive committee as well as on The Saddlery Steering Group of The Worshipful Company of Saddlers, of which she is also a Liveryman. This group is responsible for running and overseeing all British Saddlery Apprenticeships. She has trained many apprentices, all of whom have also been very successful in national competitions.

A Master Saddler at the Royal Mews, Buckingham Palace for the last 13 years, Frances now works there part time, making and renovating all types of equestrian leather items. Saddles are no longer made at the Mews, however they are all fitted to individual horses by Frances and all repairs to saddles are carried out in the Mews workshop. Together with a colleague, she specialises in renovating the State Harness for the Palace as well as for the Royal Stables in Stockholm. There are three categories of harness - Full State Harness, Semi State Harness and Exercise Harness each having different degrees of use. State Harnesses are used only a few times a year and may last for 100 years or more. Semi State Harnesses are used more often - for example, for Royal Ascot or visits of High Commissioners - and therefore require more than the usual regular maintenance.

When not in London Frances runs her own business making bridles, carriage driving harnesses and dog collars. She mainly produces made-to-measure bridles for professional show and dressage riders who have found that the off-the-peg versions do not fit so well. Professionals understand that a good bridle can very much enhance the look of the animal, and good quality leather will last longer, be easier to maintain, and be more comfortable on the hand and the horse. Ultimately, if the horse is comfortable it will perform better.

Whether for the Royal Palace or for her own business, all her bridles are finely stitched by hand using the best quality materials. There is no compromise. Her bridle straps, for example, are made from two strips of leather pared at their edges giving them a more substantial feel and look, with holes which are shaped for easy fool-proof fastening. Hand stitching is stronger than machine stitching and will give a longer trouble-free life. At the Royal Mews she showed me her tools of the trade, some interesting looking items - stuffers, smashers and stitch mark irons - each having a specific purpose. She often prefers to use old tools rather than new - specifically she prefers a stitch-mark iron made by one John Adams - now long deceased - because of its size, weight and delicate balance. In days of old, all craftsmen owned their own tools and stamped them with their name.

Sandie Lush - Quilt Maker

Sandie has been interested in crafts from an early age. She learned about quilts from her sister-in-law who introduced her to the craft of patchwork and quilting in the early 80's when she lived in the United States. Ten years later, back in England, she made a quilt for her second child, and more followed for family members. She attended classes and joined a local group of quilters. In 1993 she attended a class with Barbara Chainey who introduced her to whole-cloth quilting. Having no patchwork seams to stitch across, Sandie found this was her ideal type of quilt and was the start of her passion for hand-stitched whole-cloth quilts.

Shortly after this she attended a show where she saw quilts made by the late Amy Emms, an English quilter and teacher of renown. In due course Sandie entered a small quilt into a show and sold it. She was inspired. She decided to make a large quilt which became Champion Quilt at the Great British Quilt Festival in 1996. Next followed her signature quilt, made in the form of a giant cricket sweater measuring 40 inches by 70 inches (see photograph) created as her entry into the exhibition at Lords Cricket Ground by the Quilters' Guild of the British Isles. One of her most successful pieces, "Fantasy", gained first place at the Festival of Quilts at the National Exhibition Centre, Birmingham, in 2004, as well as winning blue ribbons at the Quilters' Heritage Celebration in Pennsylvania, the American Quilter's Society in Paducah Kentucky and the International Quilt Association in Houston, Texas. It was also the Champion quilt at Malvern in 2007. Sandie continues to exhibit regularly at national and international shows.

A quilt is generally defined as a covering consisting of three layers of material held together by stitching, although some consider the use of two layers equally acceptable. There are three broad categories: traditional, contemporary, and art. A traditional quilt is usually made for a bed and uses established techniques and designs. Contemporary quilts may be made for display on either walls or beds. They are characterised by their more fluid and unusual designs, but often are made using traditional techniques. Art quilts are free-form and always made for display on walls. Methods of design and construction may incorporate other non-textile elements and traditional techniques are often used in novel ways.

Sandie makes quilted cushions, cot, bed, lap and wall quilts. She also designs patterns and pattern books for sale. Her patterns are first sketched out on paper before being scanned into and redrawn on a computer. Before being packaged ready for sale, a sample is made of each pattern. In 2003 she contributed the section 'Whole Cloth and Hand Quilting' to the book entitled *Quilting from Start to Finish* by Katharine Guerrier.

She also teaches hand quilting and hand appliqué, makes quilts to commission, and, when she goes on holiday, Sandie loves to relax … and make quilts.

Sue Macniven - Spinner

Sue has always been interested in crafts, having grown up surrounded by a family of knitters and weavers. She was taught knitting by her mother and tatting by her aunt and, wishing to do something original within the family, she decided to take up spinning. Having never seen it done, she attended evening classes, acquired a spinning wheel and has never looked back. She is now on the speakers/tutors list for the Association of Spinners, Weavers and Dyers, teaches other spinning groups around the country, runs courses at her home in Scotland and exhibits at numerous art & craft exhibitions. In 1999 she entered the 'Longest Thread' competition held in Tasmania, entering the Guinness Book of Records as world champion with the longest unbroken 2 ply thread of 943.49m from 10 grams of wool. In 2001 she again took the record with a thread length of 1037.28m.

Spinning is the process of twisting fibres together to form a yarn and can be applied to plant, animal and synthetic fibres. Whilst Sue has spun all of these at one time or another, she now concentrates on spinning animal fibres. She spins wool from sheep although prefers the finer fibres from the angora rabbit, angora goat (mohair), and the down from camel, yak, musk ox and vicuna. The down is the soft fibre left next to the skin after the outer hair has been removed. She also spins silk as well as wool from the alpaca, the latter being bred near her home in Scotland.

A fleece is first graded to ensure the hair is a consistent length and quality, and then washed. The wool is then either combed (making the fibres all lie in one direction) or carded (which opens out the fibres, making them fluffy).

To spin the wool, a carded preparation, known as a rolag, is held in one hand, whilst the other hand pulls out some fibres and the wheel imparts a twist. This produces a twisted 'singles' thread which is then continuously wound onto the bobbin on the spinning wheel. The direction in which the yarn is spun is known as either Z (clockwise) or S (anticlockwise) spun. The tightness of twist is measured in TPI (the number of twists per inch) and the thickness as WPI (the number of wraps of yarn around a ruler per inch). The distance between the spinner's hands is determined by the length of the fibre being spun. Short draw spinning usually uses longer combed wool, ultimately giving a smooth hardwearing yarn called worsted. Long draw spinning (made using a rolag) makes a woollen yarn which is lighter and fluffier.

Microscopic inspection of the surface of animal hair reveals scales and protrusions which produce enough friction between the hairs to allow them to be spun into one continuous yarn without breaking. Single yarns may be used as spun, or plied together to form a thicker yarn. When spinning, the twist is made in one direction and the plying in the opposite direction; this balances the yarn allowing the resulting garment to hang straight without a bias twist.

Ian Middleton - Glove Maker

Ian was brought up in the countryside and has always had a very keen interest in birds. He owned an owl when he was twelve years old and they were inseparable. Ian told me he was seen in the locality as the real-life boy in the classic book Kes, who trained and practically lived with his kestrel. It was at this early age that Ian realised the importance of the falconer's glove. Now, through his company Raptor Craft Traditionals, in addition to making hand-sewn gloves, he makes other 'furniture' required by falconers such as bags, hoods and leather claw straps. He sells to discerning customers in the USA and UAE as well as in this country. He has been commissioned by museums, by re-enactment societies and has made several TV appearances.

The sport of falconry, which probably started over 3000 years ago, judging by references on tablets in the tomb of Tutankhamun, is based on the use of trained birds of prey to pursue game. In the time of Henry V111, falconry was extremely popular and glove makers were highly respected craftsmen. Ian and his partner Carole run their company Wild-Wings, where they give falconry displays, individual falconry tuition, educational talks and attend numerous events around the country.

Ian perfected his skills in glove making by trial and error. Over time he came to understand the best way of making the glove, how to cut the leather and how to hand-sew to achieve the very best fit. As a practising falconer, he intuitively knew what he wanted and what was best for the bird. Different birds require different gloves. Falcons require softer leather as their claws do not grip very tightly. Hawks on the other hand, who grip their prey in their powerful talons, require a harder, but still supple leather. Eagles need yet harder leather to cope with their powerful grip as well as a longer glove gauntlet as their legs are further apart.

Traditional falconry gloves are hand-cut from a single piece of leather using a template of four fingers; the thumb sleeve is made separately. Fawcettes (strips of leather forming the thickness of the finger sleeves) are cut and the leather hand-stitched starting from between the thumb and the forefinger and sewing continuously to the end of the little finger. He uses a tri-sided needle, trimming the leather from time to time to achieve the perfect shape to give maximum comfort. Most gloves are made to fit the left hand, leaving the right hand free to feed the bird, remove the hood or to carry out other manipulations. Gloves are often lined; some in warm fleece, others in cotton. Some customers require summer and winter gloves having different insulation properties; others require specific decoration. In other cases Ian decorates the gloves as he feels appropriate. He uses elk leather from Scandinavia, which is soft and of high quality. More recently he has used kudo, leather from the African antelope.

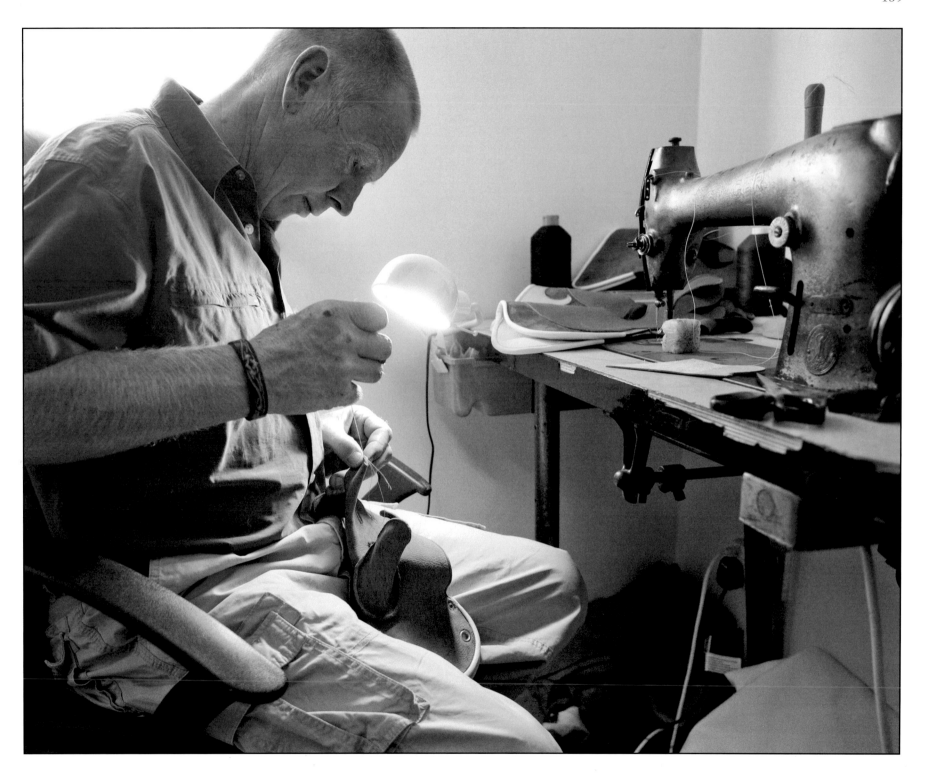

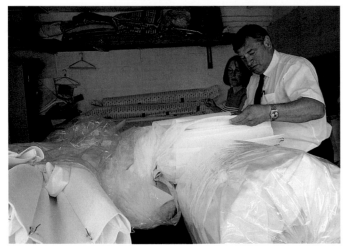

Bottom: Stephen Chapman, Managing Director

Stephen Mills - Upholsterer

Stephen Mills works for the family firm of Albert E Chapman Limited, soft furnishers and upholsterers. The company was founded in 1931 and is now managed by Albert's grandson, Stephen Chapman, who, like his father (Bertram) before him, is a Liveryman and Court Assistant of the Worshipful Company of Upholders.

Stephen Mills learnt his craft at college and in other companies before moving to Albert E Chapman Limited 18 years ago where he is now Senior Upholsterer. As well as being an active upholsterer, Stephen oversees all the upholstery work. He frequently works on the Royal ceremonial carriages and, over the years, Chapman's have restored the upholstery on many of these vehicles, most recently making a new hammer cloth for the Glass Coach used for the State Opening of Parliament in 2010. The company also carries out work for English Heritage. Interior designers remain the largest customer base.

Albert E Chapman Limited is a traditional upholstery company; most of its work comprises re-dressing (re-covering) chairs, settees, four-poster beds and installing stretched-fabric wallcoverings. The company was engaged in the dressing of Westminster Hall in 1935 for the ceremony to mark the Silver Jubilee of King George V and again, in January 1936, for his Lying-In-State.

In 1988, Albert E Chapman Limited was appointed 'into the place and quality of Upholsterers to Her Majesty the Queen'. This was later extended to 'the place and quality of Upholsterers and Soft Furnishers'. The company is a member of the Association of Upholsterers & Soft-Furnishers. Both Stephen and Bertram Chapman are Directors.

Albert E Chapman Limited is recognised within the upholstery and re-upholstery industry as leading exponents of traditional upholstery. The craftsmen are well versed in techniques used in the 17th Century with variations and developments up to the present day. They can therefore carry out conservation, restoration or complete re-upholstery work, using appropriate materials, whatever the nature of the item.

Pat Perryman - Lace Maker

Forty one years ago Pat was persuaded by a friend to join a local lace making class in Honiton. Two and a half years later she was conducting the class. A dressmaker by trade, Pat is now the chairman of the Allhallows Museum of Lace in Honiton, home to the most comprehensive collection in the world. She lectures locally, nationally and internationally; has appeared on TV, including being an invited specialist on The Antiques Road show, and is the co-author of the definitive book *New Designs in Honiton Lace*. Pat was commissioned to make the jabot and cuffs for the Parliamentary robes for the Speaker of the House of Commons, and also several pieces to commemorate major royal events.

Before 1810 all lace was hand-made, with Honiton being established as an important centre since the 16th century. The local resources were excellent. There was a good supply of raw materials (flax was grown nearby in Axminster) and transport (it was on the main route to London).

Honiton lace is characterised by being a 'part lace', that is, the various motifs and other small pieces could be made by different lace makers and then joined together to make the larger finished product. Many workers could contribute, thus enabling commercial quantities to be produced.

The two main techniques for making lace use either bobbins or a needle, although crochet hooks or knitting needles are also used. Honiton lace is made using the bobbin technique. This is essentially a process of weaving very fine threads which are wound onto bobbins; typically the thread is 2 ply 120 Egyptian cotton, (about one-third the thickness of sewing cotton). Making a piece of lace using this technique first requires a drawing which is transferred to a piece of card known as the pricking. This card is placed onto a firm pillow packed with barley straw; holes are pricked in it at regular close intervals along every line of the design. The threads are fixed at the start of the pattern, although more can be added, or removed, as the work progresses. All the stitches use two pairs of bobbins, that is, four threads. Once a stitch has been made it is held in position with a pin pushed through the pin-hole in the pricking. The pattern motifs, which can be outlined with a gimp (a thicker thread), are usually worked in cloth stitch (forming areas resembling woven cloth), or half stitch (giving a more open effect), although more elaborate filling stitches may also be used.

Bobbin lace can be worked in two different ways. In straight lace the motifs and ground of meshes or bars are made in one continuous process. In part lace the motifs are made separately and then joined with bars or a mesh ground. Once the lace is finished it is released from the pattern by removing the pins.

Eleanor Pritchard
Wool Weaver

Eleanor trained at the Chelsea College of Art and Design; now part of what is known as the University of the Arts incorporating several London colleges. On leaving college she became self-employed and was fortunate to be entered into a competition to be selected to show her work at a trade show in Paris. As a result she obtained her first commission: to weave some fabric for Christian Lacroix. She has never looked back. Her work is represented in London by Margaret Howell, and she also has items on display at shops such as Liberty. She was featured as part of Fortnum and Mason's 2010 exhibition entitled 'Handmade', which celebrated the best of British craft. Eleanor exhibits at trade shows to meet potential clients; it was through this route she secured a commission to design and weave a number of large panels for the new National Trust headquarters in Swindon. She also attends the biennial New York International Gift Fair.

She has recently had a major exhibition 'Place Setting' at the Orleans House Gallery in Twickenham and is currently working on designs for the magazine 'Wallpaper' who are exhibiting at the furniture trade show in Milan and on a commission for a new set of ceremonial robes for Ely Cathedral. She is frequently featured in magazines and is an associate lecturer at Central Saint Martins, teaching part of the Textile Design course.

All her design work, sampling and bespoke hand-weaving is carried out at her studio in South East London. Eleanor uses a manual Dobby loom and works predominantly in wool sourced from Scotland. Like most weavers these days much of her non-commissioned work is hand-sampled; that is, the prototype is woven by hand and the commercial product then woven by a specialist mill. For production runs Eleanor uses the Cambrian mill in Wales.

A love of pattern, colour and texture runs through all of her work. Her designs frequently reflect her love of the countryside but she is also influenced by everyday objects, such as the '405' and '625 ranges of blankets based on the TV standard lines/inch - '405' being in black and white, and '625' in colour (see illustration). Her palette is influenced by the soft chalky colours of early to mid 20th century English painters such as Ben and E Q Nicholson, Stanley Spencer and Eric Ravilious.

Heather Richie - Rug Maker

When she moved to Yorkshire some 40 years ago, Heather bought her first house but had no money left for carpets. A visiting farmer's wife suggested that she could make rugs to keep out the draughts using the same materials used by local farmers - old sacks and torn up stockings. Having always been busy either sewing or knitting she was fascinated, and made the rugs as suggested. She is now a prolific rug maker and has moved from making 'useful' rugs to rugs as pieces of art with many intended as wall hangings. Her designs always tell a story, either of her life or of the life around her. For example, she has a rug showing herself as a small child, leading her father, who became blind when she was six, along the street to count the number of steps between lamp posts. Another well publicised rug shows five old men chatting in a bus shelter in her village; sadly all the men have now died, but their memory lives on in Heather's work.

Heather uses two rug making techniques known as 'Hooky' and 'Proddy'. Hooky uses long pieces of fabric on the wrong side of the hessian base, pulled through to the right side to create a series of loops which form the design. Proddy is essentially the reverse, pushing small pieces of fabric from the underside to form a shaggy pile on the right side. Heather often mixes two techniques in the same rug.

A breakthrough came when she was commissioned to make two rugs for the artist Mackenzie Thorpe which were copies of his pictures. He later sold the rugs for a considerable sum and kindly gave Heather a further payment which she used to enable her to attend a rug making school in Vermont. Unknown to Heather at the time was the fact that of her two rug making techniques, the Americans used only Hooky. They were enthralled and invited her back to give tuition. She now runs rug making courses in the USA twice yearly as well as numerous courses in this country.

In 2004, Heather and her daughter, who works with blind people, made a visit to Zanzibar and were appalled by the poverty, and that blind people were forced to beg on the streets. She thought that, although blind, people could learn to make rugs as a potential source of income and decided to give a demonstration. 50 people arrived and, by the end of the day, all could make a basic rug despite neither speaking the other's language. By the simple method of holding their hands they soon learned the basic techniques. On her return to England she set up a not-for-profit organisation 'Rug-Aid' with the aim of providing opportunities for children and women in some of poorest countries in Africa. In 2007 she went to the resource centre of the Gambian Organisation for the Visually Impaired in Serrekunda and, with support from Sightsavers International, carried out a similar and successful feasibility study. Whilst none of her students can read or write, each rug is labelled with the maker's name and fingerprint.

Ingrid Sixsmith - Tapestry Maker

Having left school at sixteen, Ingrid enrolled at college five years later to study textiles. In the second year of her degree she studied woven textiles but did not find them stimulating; when making tapestry however, she realised she had found her future. Her view is that whereas fabrics feature patterns, tapestries depict pictures - thus they can tell a story; they have something to say. Ingrid has something to say and she communicates her thoughts and views through her work. Her woven pictures convey spiritual ideas, ecological views and events in the world around her. When I visited, she was nearing the completion of her latest work entitled 'Fat Cats', a satirical look at the 'Banker's Bonus' scandal. Although she usually works to commission, this was a speculative piece which, in her view, "asked to be woven"; however, she hopes to find a buyer.

A member of the British Tapestry Group, Ingrid usually makes large contemporary pieces taking many months to complete. She works using a 1.5m wide floor loom, weaving tapestries anything up to 6m in length. She has had many commissions, including tapestries for two cruise liners, for several major international companies and numerous hospitals. Colours are very important to Ingrid; she chooses them carefully to be in keeping with the subject matter; a hospital scene, for example, should have calming colours, never red.

The starting point is a picture which Ingrid paints on canvas. This picture is then copied by hand using a grid system onto a full sized sheet of paper marked out to show the image boundaries and the different colours - this is called the cartoon. The cartoon is then cut into horizontal strips about 25cm high and placed immediately behind the warped loom. In this way, Ingrid can mark each thread to show the general outline of the picture. With the cartoon strip in the background as a constant reminder of the colours, weaving can commence. Ingrid uses cotton for both the warp and the weft. She uses 7 strands for each thread, which may comprise a number of different colours. The threads, which are several feet long, are rolled up and tied in a bow - known as a butterfly - to avoid ravelling. There may be up to 50 different butterflies in use at any one time. The weaving is painstaking work and frequent breaks are needed to avoid strain. Long tapestries require a disciplined approach and a 2 hour on with 2 hour break regime is often adopted. It is not surprising therefore that the end of weaving demands a celebration and the 'cutting off' ceremony is justly a social occasion. The final stage is to sew all the hundreds of thread ends on the reverse of the tapestry to the warp.

Bottom: Michael Sowden Jn.

Michael Sowden
Violin Bow Hair Dresser

At the age of fifteen Michael started working as a horse hair dresser in a small Yorkshire village, dressing horse hair to make a wide range of brushes and other products, including horse hair for use in violin and cello bows. Following competition from hair and bristle merchants abroad, in 1994 he decided to concentrate on the horse hair dressing part of the business, producing only bow hair. Michael and his son Michael junior run the company and have 1468 customers in 46 countries. They believe they are the only suppliers of quality bow hair for professional musicians in Europe and possibly the world.

In general only white horse tail hair is used, although some double-bass players prefer the slightly thicker and stronger black hair. Only the tail from the mare is used, identified by the urine stain at the tapered end.

The secret of their success is quality, supplying only the very best hair. This means inspecting every part of every hair for defects. These may be kinked, curly or chalky, the latter referring to a condition where the hair is brittle or may stretch but not return to its original length, a condition associated with poor nutrition. Michael obtains his hair from Canada and Mongolia. In Mongolia the large groups of horses are a form of currency and are well looked after. After 6-7 years they are slaughtered for food. Everything else is a by-product.

Following a tightening of Health and Safety regulations some years ago the import of unwashed hair was banned. Washed and disinfected hair is now received in one kilogram bundles, with approximately 33000 hairs per bundle.

After sorting the colours, each bundle is drawn repeatedly through the hackle (vertical spikes) to allow all the hairs to separate. Then begins the first of three main operations. In the first, known as the first way dressing, bundles of hair are tied at one end and cut square. Up to 20 such bundles are laid flat on the bench and anchored in such a way as to allow individual hairs to be withdrawn. By using a specially made tool, the longest hairs are drawn out, these being in the range 40-42 inches. This is followed by withdrawing those of length 30-35 inches, then 27-30 inches. The latter is used for weaving; those less than 27 inches are used for items such as judge's wigs and sporrans. The second way dressing is a similar operation except that the range of lengths is reduced to one half an inch. The third stage is to inspect the whole length of each hair for defects, at which point up to 40% may be rejected. Finally the hair is weighed and tied into bundles of the required weight. For Mongolian hair blue cord is used with loops every three inches. For Canadian hair, green cord is used.

Hazel Tindall - Knitter

Hazel has no memory of having been taught to knit; her grandmother and mother were accomplished knitters, so it was natural that they would pass on their skills to the children. Many years ago, every home in Shetland had at least one person who knitted; visitors brought their knitting and garments were sold, particularly to customers from abroad. Things changed in the early 1970s when North Sea oil came ashore to the terminal at Sullom Voe, a few miles from Hazel's home. The industry offered jobs to local people and the social infrastructure changed. Not only was there an abundance of paid work, but this also brought companionship rather than the isolation of knitting alone at home. In recent years there has been a resurgence in the popularity of hand knitting although nowadays it is more of a hobby than an industry.

In 2004 Hazel became the 'world's fastest knitter' in a contest organised in London by the UK Hand Knitting Association. The previous year, Hazel and her friends had found an internet reference to the fact that the then champion knitter had achieved 180 stitches in three minutes. They thought they could do better and promptly did so at home. Hazel was duly put forward for the competition and won with 255 stitches in three minutes and, through sponsorship, raised funds for The Shetland Textile Working Museum. In 2008 the Craft Yarn Council of America held the championship in Minnesota and again Hazel won, bettering her previous record with 262 stitches per three minutes. In both competitions knitters worked on 60 stitches. In London there was only one timed session; stocking stitch (alternate rows of knit and purl) was knitted on 4mm needles, and a knitting belt was allowed. In America there were three timed sessions, using 5mm needles and garter stitch (no purl).

She believes that it is important to have good technique, containing finger movements into a very small area. She likes to use thin (2-3mm) double pointed knitting needles with a knitting belt, which helps to stabilise the needle. Hazel generally knits Fair Isle - using two colours across each row to create geometric shapes. She almost always uses wool from Shetland sheep farmed in Shetland as she likes the way the wool handles. Using undyed wool restricts her colour palette to the colours of the sheep - fawns, browns, greys and black. For greater variety, she uses dyed wool too but finds garments (she rarely knits decorative items) knitted from undyed wool are warmer.

Hazel rarely follows commercial knitting patterns, preferring to design her own sweaters. From her collection of graphed shapes, she chooses which to use, depending on the size and shape of the garment to be knitted, and how complex she wants to make it. Years of experience has given her the confidence to knit whole garments without knitting swatches to decide on how to use colours. Her ambition is to pass on her skills to a younger generation.

Rachel Trevor-Morgan - Milliner

From an early age, Rachel's ambition was to become an actress and this developed into a keen interest in theatre costume. It is from this sense of the dramatic, coupled with her mother's love of hats, that Rachel's passion for millinery evolved. During a year in London, and considering her future, she contacted various milliners with a view to pursuing her interest. The industry was small and people knew each other. Rachel was offered an apprenticeship with Graham Smith: he offered a rigorous training in the disciplined craft of millinery whilst maintaining the individuality of design and flawless finish which are central to its art. This background has given Rachel a strong base in couture millinery where each hat is hand blocked and stitched and every flower hand dyed and rolled.

In 1990 Rachel established her own business which she operates from her 17th century atelier in St James's, London. From here she makes hats for private clients, each one of which is bespoke. Every aspect of the hat or headpiece is entirely hand made from start to finish. All of Rachel's trimmings are made in-house in order to keep an individual feel to the hats and ensure that customers have a unique piece. When a customer comes to the showroom they normally bring in their outfit or colour swatches; many different styles are tried on to find the best hat for them.

Rachel uses many different fabrics for her hats. Each one is made on a wooden form using a process called blocking. This is the shaping of the raw material, which may be felt, or straw or a foundation material which is later covered in a fabric. The blocked shape is then stiffened to maintain the shape; this is then worked upon to create the hat. The final stage is the trimming, using materials such as feathers and flowers. This final stage has endless possibilities, limited only by imagination and, of course, the consideration of the wearer and occasion on which it is to be worn. Rachel's success is rooted in her lifelong passion for the craft of millinery and her understanding of the balance required for a hat to flatter and to be the finishing touch to an outfit.

Following the retirement of Royal milliner Frederick Fox, new British talent was sought and in 2006 Rachel was asked to submit sketches of her work for consideration. Her designs were successful and Rachel was appointed Milliner to the Queen. Her first Royal commission was worn on the occasion of Her Majesty's 80th birthday celebration and this has been followed by many others for high profile occasions such as Royal Ascot. Rachel also designs hats for other members of the Royal family. She is a Liveryman of the Worshipful Company of Feltmakers and is now responsible for organising the Annual Feltmakers design award for apprentices and students.

Rachel's hats are works of art. Her style is feminine, glamorous, elegant and always flattering.

Wim Visscher - Vellum Maker

Bottom: Spencer McRickus

William Cowley Ltd is one of the world's leading manufacturers of quality vellums and parchments. The company has been in continuous production since 1870 in the small market town of Newport Pagnell and is the only producer of vellum in the UK. The business is now managed by Wim Visscher, a fourth generation member of the family who has been with the company for many years and has an intimate practical knowledge of every stage in the production. Little has changed, the same techniques being used today as when the company was formed. Wim trains his staff in every aspect of production; it takes many years to master the craft of making parchment. Several people have spent their entire working lives with the firm.

Parchment is the generic name for thin material made from calfskin, sheepskin or goatskin. It is produced by skilled craftsman using traditional methods and is used for documents. Although the best quality parchment is called vellum (from the French word for calf - velin) made from calfskin, the name is now generally applied regardless of which skin is used. Parchment is distinct from leather in that it is limed, but not tanned; thus it is not waterproof and is affected by changes in humidity.

The skins are first soaked in lime for some days following which they are scraped in the beam house to remove the hair, flesh and other unwanted material - this is very messy work! They are then bleached and washed in lime to render them supple before being stretched on individual frames. Once on the frames, the skins are again lime washed and scraped until the desired thickness has been achieved. They are then left to dry for a few days - a very critical stage - followed by several further controlled drying stages before being finally ready for sale.

Calf skin generally produces the highest quality vellum and is the preferred material on which to write; the surface also makes it easier to erase any writing should this be necessary. It is slightly thicker than that made from goatskin or sheepskin, the latter being thinner due to the need to remove more fatty material during manufacture.

All Acts of Parliament have been recorded on vellum since 1497 and are held in the House of Lords. In 1849 it was decreed that two copies of each would be made, a practice that continues to this day. Vellum is also used for calligraphy, heraldic painting, bookbinding, certificates ... and drumheads. One of the most notable uses of vellum supplied by William Cowley in recent years was for the hand-written and illuminated Saint John's Bible completed in 2008 by Donald Jackson.

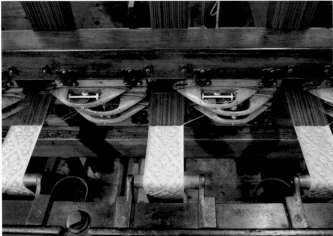

Neil Warburton- Narrow Fabric Weaver

Neil and his wife Anna operate Context Weavers, a weaving business specialising in the reproduction of historic fabrics, but Neil's particular passion is the weaving of 'small wares'; that is, silk ribbons, tapes and ornate braids. Like many things in life, his career in textiles was accidental. While living in London in the 1960's - Neil and Anna were typical 'hippies' of the swinging sixties - he knew a shop in Knightsbridge selling and repairing oriental carpets. He became fascinated by the small table-top loom which was used to make small pieces of carpet, and bought the loom (for £8), acquired a book from the library and taught himself the basics of weaving.

In the mid 70's Neil and Anna moved north and bought a house in the 'Heavy Woollen District' about 7 miles from Leeds. At that time, the textile mills were closing down and weaving equipment could be bought very cheaply. In their small terraced house they installed a loom in the front room, another in the bedroom, and one in the garden shed, putting a winder in the kitchen. Neil had acquired the weaving 'bug' and developed an obsession for weaving which continues to this day. He was single-minded - not wanting the standard textile course at college - just wanting to learn how to weave. He came to an arrangement with Huddersfield Polytechnic where he was allowed to weave with the principal lecturer. As master and apprentice they tackled the entire range of weaving skills, warping, winding, drawing in and weaving. So Neil came to acquire the essential knowledge of weaving.

After a degree in textile design at Leeds University Anna joined the textile museum in Helmshore in Lancashire and this is where they are still settled. It was here that they began their weaving business, with Anna designing and Neil weaving. Initially Neil wove 'tourist goods' such as scarves and table place-mats. He was asked if he could produce a half-inch silk ribbon to be used on the Duke of Wellington's chair at Aspley House in London. Neil accepted the commission and sometime later the chair featured in a slide show by the Furniture History Society at the Victoria and Albert Museum. It caught the attention of some members of the National Trust and thus commenced a long association with the Trust.

At their premises at Park Mill in Helmshore they now have a wide range of different looms. This collection of machinery enables Neil to weave a diverse range of fabrics from a 1/4in silk tape to heavy tapestry carpet at 27in wide. In addition Neil and Anna collect antique looms and have written a booklet *Looms and Weaving* for the Shire Series of Albums.

Neil showed me around the mill where 100 year old power looms were working alongside newer machines. He has one department full of specialist narrow fabric looms and was setting these up to weave braid for the restoration of vintage cars. Neil considers this 'carriage lace' to be one of the most complex and challenging of narrow fabrics and is now adding this to the wide range of ribbons and braids he weaves for museums, palaces and historic houses.

Top: Richard Farrow inspecting the leather for 2nd quality control.
Centre: Paul Wilkinson, Shaving Machine Operator.
Bottom: Mark Mason, Finishing Shop Operator.

David Winstone - Currier

David Winstone is one of a team of four trained curriers working for J & E Sedgwick & Co, leather suppliers. He has been with the company for eleven years, having served his apprenticeship under Richard Farrow, the Managing Director.

The company was founded by James and Emmanuel Sedgwick in 1900. In the 1920's Richard Farrow, grandfather of the present Richard, was seeking to leave farming in which he saw little future, and joined the company. In due course, James and Emmanuel retired and the company was managed by Richard senior, but, by agreement, the name was retained. It is still a family business; Richard's son Shaun being the Marketing Director. Richard has trained and worked in every part of the business, including the key craft of currying, and both father and son are members of the Worshipful Company of Curriers. From the very beginning the company supplied leather to the equestrian trade and more than a century later is still one of the leading suppliers of equestrian leather in the country.

Currying is the name given to the process of stretching and finishing tanned leather, thus making it into a pliant workable material. It is then ready for other craftsmen to use in making a wide variety of leather goods. It is the key process in the production of quality leather. The word 'currier' is believed to be derived from the Latin term 'corium'. The corium is the central skin layer between the outer epidermis and the flesh underneath, made up of a complex series of fibres. The composition of this layer dictates the difference in texture between leathers. The currier essentially scrapes both sides of the hide – the outer side with a flat metal blade, known as a 'sleeker'; the inner side with a currying knife. The blade of this knife is at right angles to the handle, thus enabling it to be worked like a wood plane, shaving the surface of the leather. Currying the hide by hand allows the currier to scrape in any direction, as opposed to a machine that is necessarily unidirectional; thus the hand working of the leather will produce a consistently superior surface quality.

Sedgwicks use hides from locally farmed, well fed prime beef cattle, the high quality husbandry producing a superior hide, and ultimately, the best leather. Tanned hides entering the factory are carefully inspected before being mechanically split and graded to the required thickness; different thicknesses being destined for different products - saddles are made from 5mm thick leather, other luxury goods such as handbags and wallets use a thickness of 1.5mm. After surface cleaning the leather is retanned to make it supple and workable, before being curried by hand to ensure the grain is smooth and correctly set. Further quality checks are made before it is hand stained and given a final application of grease. Only then is it ready for the customer, the whole process taking 18 weeks to complete.

Index by Name

Index by Name

Index by Occupation

Index by Occupation

Contact Information

Mike Abbott	Greenwood worker	Worcestershire	www.living-wood.co.uk
Norman Ackroyd	Etcher and engraver	London	www.normanackroyd.com
Bruce Aitken	Clock maker	Derbyshire	www.bruceaitken-clockmaker.co.uk
Jeremy Atkinson	Clog maker	Herefordshire	www.clogmaker.co.uk
Tim Baker	Violin bow maker	Oxfordshire	www.bvma.org.uk
David Bamford	Carpet designer and colourist	Powys	www.davidbamfordhandmadecarpets.com
Jan Beaney	Textile artist	Berkshire	www.doubletrouble.com
Nina Bilbey	Stone carver	Norfolk	www.ninabilbey.com
Katherine Brett	Marbled paper maker	Cambridgeshire	www.payhembury.com
Simon Brett	Wood engraver	Wiltshire	www.simonbrett-woodengraver.co.uk
Martin Buckle	Bee skep maker	Bedfordshire	www.martinatnewton.com
Seumas Campbell	Dry stone dyker	Isle of Skye	email: seumasc@tiscali.co.uk
Deborah Carré	Shoe maker	London	www.carreducker.com
Nicky Clacy	Papier-mâché artist	Yorkshire	www.papiermachesculptures.co.uk
Heather Coleman	Clay pipe maker	Devon	www.dawnmist.demon.co.uk
Emmanuel Cooper	Potter	London	email: emmanuelcooper@lineone.net
Anna Crutchley	Passementerie maker	Cambridgeshire	email: a.crutchley@ntlworld.com
Joan Cutts	Egg crafter	Northumberland	email: joancutts@aol.com
Chris Daunt	Wood block maker	Northumberland	www.chrisdaunt.com
Anthony Dew	Rocking horse maker	Yorkshire	www.rockinghorse.co.uk
Chris Drury	Artist	Sussex	www.chrisdrury.co.uk
James Ducker	Shoe maker	London	www.carreducker.com
Hugh Dunford Wood	Wallpaper maker	Dorset	www.handmadewallpaper.co.uk

Contact Information

Chris Elmer	Wood sculptor	Gloucestershire	www.chriselmersculpture.co.uk
Christoph Götting	Violin maker	Hampshire	www.gottingviolins.co.uk
Tom Hare	Willow artist	Leicestershire	www.tomharewillowman.com
Julian Hart	Silversmith	Gloucestershire	www.hartsilversmiths.co.uk
Sean Henry	Sculptor	Wiltshire	www.seanhenry.com
Darrell Hill	Willow coffin maker	Somerset	www.willowcoffins.co.uk
Bob Hobbs	Blacksmith	Somerset	(contact details witheld)
Robert Hurford	Wheelwright	Somerset	www.chariotmaker.co.uk
Charles Hutcheon	Stick maker	Sussex	email: c.hutcheon@lineone.net
Donald Jackson	Calligrapher	Monmouthshire	www.saintjohnsbible.org
Michael Johnson	Copper worker	Cornwall	www.thecopperworksnewlyn.com
Graham Jones	Tree carver	Warwickshire	www.gmjwoodcarving.co.uk
Owen Jones	Oak swill basket maker	Cumbria	www.oakswills.co.uk
Peter Jones	Charcoal maker	Kent	tel: 01303 893401
Jim Keeling	Potter	Warwickshire	www.whichfordpottery.com
Frances Kelly	Saddler	Berkshire	www.franceskellybridles.co.uk
Terry Kenny	Coracle maker	Shropshire	www.coraclemaker.co.uk
Adam King	Besom broom maker	Buckinghamshire	www.adamking.co.uk
Terry King	Photographer	Surrey	www.hands-on-pictures.com
Richard Lewis	Hedge layer	Powys	tel: 01597 824355
Shaun Linsley	Cane fishing rod maker	Dorset	email: shaunlinsley@yahoo.com
John Lord	Flint knapper	Norfolk	www.flintknapping.co.uk
Sandie Lush	Quilt maker	Gloucestershire	www.sandielush.co.uk

Contact Information

Sue Macniven	Spinner	Dumfries & Galloway	www.handspun-exotics.com
Ronald Maddox	Watercolour painter	Hertfordshire	tel: 01438 714884
John Makepeace	Furniture designer and maker	Dorset	www.johnmakepeacefurniture.com
Mike Manns	Fletcher	Leicestershire	www.bowyersandfletchersguild.org
Bernard Middleton	Bookbinder and restorer	London	(contact details withheld)
Ian Middleton	Glove maker	Lancashire	email: raptorcraft@hotmail.co.uk
Rod Miller	Thatcher	Dorset	www.rodmiller.co.uk
Stephen Mills	Upholsterer	London	www.albertechapman.co.uk
Stuart Mortimer	Wood turner	Hampshire	www.stuartmortimer.com
Stephen Mottram	Marionettist	Oxfordshire	email: stephen.mottram@virgin.net
Alan Mudd	Enameller	Norfolk	email: mekalyst@btinternet.com
James Mursell	Windsor chair maker	Sussex	www.thewindsorworkshop.co.uk
Lawrence Neal	Rush seated chair maker	Warwickshire	www.lawrencenealchairs.co.uk
Carl Nordbruch	Glass artist	Isle of Wight	email: carlnordbruch@rocketmail.com
Gillian Nott	Straw craftsman	Cornwall	email: gillian@bejowan.co.uk
Joseph Nuttgens	Stained glass window artist	Buckinghamshire	www.josephnuttgens.co.uk
Jim Patterson	Paper maker	Buckinghamshire	www.thepapertrail.org.uk
Ronald Pennell	Glass engraver	Herefordshire	www.pennell.org.uk
Tom Perkins	Letter designer and carver	Cambridgeshire	www.tomperkins-lettercarving.co.uk
Pat Perryman	Lace maker	Devon	www.honitonmuseum.co.uk
Roy Pettitt	Raised engraver	Sussex	www.pandsengraving.co.uk
Eleanor Pritchard	Wool weaver	London	www.eleanorpritchard.com

Contact Information

John Randle	Letterpress printer	Gloucestershire	www.whittingtonpress.com
Derek Richards	Decoy duck maker	Somerset	www.derekrichardsdecoys.com
Heather Richie	Rug maker	Yorkshire	www.rugmaker.co.uk
Alan Rogers	Bowyer	Leicestershire	www.bowyersandfletchersguild.org
Graeme Rudd	Rake maker	Cumbria	email: johnjruddandson@btinternet.com
John Rudd	Rake maker	Cumbria	email; johnjruddandson@btinternet.com
Alastair Simms	Cooper	Wiltshire	www.wadworth.co.uk
Ingrid Sixsmith	Tapestry maker	London	www.ingridsixsmith.com
Brian Skilton	Raised engraver	Sussex	www.pandsengraving.co.uk
Michael Sowden	Bow hair dresser	Yorkshire	www.sowden.co.uk
Alan Spittle	Stonemason	Wiltshire	tel: 0750 0080 671
Olwen Tarrant	Oil painter and sculptor	Worcestershire	www.olwentarrant.co.uk
Hazel Tindall	Knitter	Shetland	email: hjtindall@yahoo.co.uk
Rachel Trevor-Morgan	Milliner	London	www.racheltrevormorgan.com
Jim Turley	Brick maker	Gloucestershire	www.colefordbrick.co.uk
Aasha Tyrrell	Gilder	London	www.carversandgilders.com
Wim Visscher	Vellum maker	Buckinghamshire	email: enquiries@williamcowley.co.uk
Neil Warburton	Narrow fabric weaver	Lancashire	email: contextweavers@hotmail.co.uk
David Winstone	Currier	Warwickshire	www.je-sedgwick.co.uk
Peter White	Marqueteer	Kent	email: peter@marquetry.org
Anastasia Young	Jeweller	London	www.anastasiayoung.co.uk

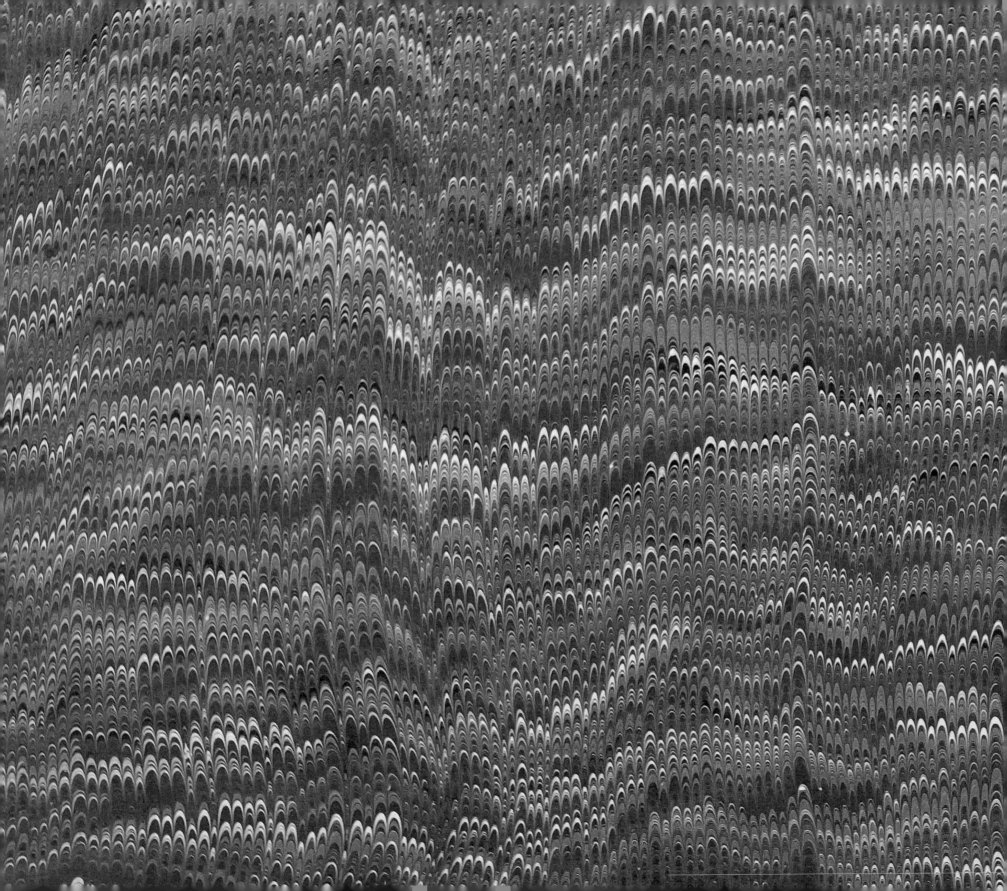